MW01118328

Beyond the Fringes

The soul of the wounded cries for help.

Janet Muthmann

*If I could just touch
The fringe of His robe.*

*Then Jesus reached out
And embraced me with His love.*

*Behold, He is here
For the needy and lame.*

Janet W. Muthmann
Ps. 118:23-24

xulon
PRESS

Comments from recent readers of <u>Beyond the Fringes</u>

'This book is needed. It addresses the deep suffering of dealing with any type of affliction in a family member. In my own it was a mental handicap, mental illness and suicide. I attached myself to the emotion and healing Janet expresses so well in her close walk with Christ and learned about life. You will be blessed.'   Martha Lynch

'An inspiring journal, documenting the author's faith in and dependence upon our Lord in all life's circumstances, both joyful and tragic. Filled with passages from Scripture, included in the accounts of the people of this family through the years, this book could be used as a 'daily devotional'.'
                                        Mary Dale Hausmann

'This book will be an inspiration to anyone who reads it.'
                                                    Rita Hall

'Jan lovingly guides us to see that every life God creates is, by His grace, able to fulfill their purpose in life. Her perseverance through tragedy gives us peace and hope. Beautifully written and illustrated.'   Gay Hall

'How does one cope when losing a child whose life is cut short according to earthy measurements? Here is a fascinating study of trust in darkest times; an autobiography of a woman's unshakeable faith in a Sovereign God who gives and Who also takes away. Throughout this book we see tremendous insights into Biblical truths. The author's solid relationship with Jesus is apparent as the reader gains great encouragement from personal applications gleaned from Scripture. To glorify God in the midst of tragedy and suffering is the greatest gift we can give back to our Creator. When do we 'consider it all joy'? When the sun shines brightest and the path is clearly illuminated? Or when in an instant our well-ordered life is changed? This riveting account of one woman's courageous journey to glorify God in the midst of trials, is so relatable one can hardly put it down. I would heartily recommend it to anyone who has suffered trials, or is now in the midst of them, or may be facing them in the future.

Delores Cole

To Juergen

In love,
In caring,
In sharing
Two shall be one.

To Our Children
Robert Reid and Shiona Ann

You came to us without knowing what our
Father had planned for you to accomplish,
yet you listened and stayed faithful to His call.
Unaware, you sent your parents on a Treasure Hunt!
I want you to know that your Dad and I continue
to thank our Father and His Son Jesus Christ
for every way He has touched our
hearts through both of you.

Acknowledgements and Thanks

Some special people have been Fragment Gathering. I want to acknowledge them and the work they so faithfully carried through to the finish. You've been faithful in praying, wiping tears, sorting bits and pieces, putting fragments in orderly fashion, holding a hand, making coffee, and offering all kinds of refreshment for the tummy and for the soul! All the labor and hours, encouragement and love have been received with gratefulness and thanks to each and to our Father, Who sees all, and rewards all.

My thanks go to these dear friends; Marty Lynch, Dale Hausmann, Ken and Glenda Mitchell, Neil and Debbie Vosburgh, Tom and Doris Landers, Dave and Linda Funk, Karen Rogeburgh, Margaret McHugh, and the ladies in the Sherwood Bible Study group. There also have been people I have not met, who have read pages and offered suggestions. I feel deeply honored to have each of you be part of this book, a Bundle of Fragments, and you have honored me by your willingness to "Gather up the Fragments that nothing be lost." God bless you for every kind word, labor, and deed.

Table of Contents
Italics indicate poetry

PSALM 139 : 13, 14, 16

FOR THOU DIDST FORM MY INWARD PARTS; THOU DIDST WEAVE ME IN MY MOTHER'S WOMB. I WILL GIVE THANKS TO THEE, FOR I AM FEARFULLY AND WONDERFULLY MADE, AND IN THY BOOK, THEY WERE WRITTEN, THE DAYS THAT WERE ORDAINED, FOR ME.

BELONG TO YOU

To My Father

You've shown the Way to blessings untold,
Yes, blessings and treasures, even secrets to behold.

Stunned, jarred and shaken, yet met by surprise;
Out of plowing and digging did these lessons arise.
When my shoes got so muddy, You said, "Holy Ground!"
"The lessons of life have been known to resound."

Thoughts laid to paper by pencil or ink
Have captured some moments I love to rethink!
Now unclasp my holding to things that are Thine,
What You have given, I shall never call mine.

You are the Source, Thou Master of thought.
Save only the good, that echoes Your thought.
Yes, blessings and treasures, as Your love You unfold,
To know You, My Father, to Whom I belong,
Who calls me by name: This Treasure Thou Art!

ALL MY WAYS ARE BEFORE THEE

Janet Muthmann

Psalm 119:168

Chapter One

In the Beginning . . .

. . . But God Knew

W hat a great resting place are these words! In the beginning God knew! There is never a beginning without God. There is no Faith without God. There is no Love without God. There is no Peace without God. It follows that we do not want to live without God. We do not want to die without God. He is the best reason for living.

These are the reasons I would never be able to write this book without God. They form the foundation for my writing about what has happened in our family. We are taught to share the comfort as He has comforted us. Did we know what lay ahead? Not at all—underlined! But God knew. He *is always there* even when we are shocked beyond words.

As I go back in my memory file, the Lord has shown me the many times and various ways in which we were prepared. No, we were not thinking "this is preparation." We were not "knowing" what He was doing; and had no indication for what we were being prepared. Thank God we were able to retain, perhaps not always implementing, but nevertheless keeping the treasures hidden in our hearts. Perhaps we only thought of certain scriptures as road marks and guideposts along the way as we are told in His Word (Jeremiah 31:21).

But He enjoys bringing all these things together at the right time, which prompts us to thank and glorify Him.

Take special notice and care of the Words the Lord points out to you because He is building in you a reservoir for His future use; things that He would like to bring to your mind at special times and for special reasons. These are your unique and distinct possessions. Here is a quote from Corrie ten Boom on God's preparation for our future usefulness:

> "Today I know that memories are the key not to the past, but to the future. I know that the experiences of our lives, when we let God use them, become the mysterious and perfect preparation for the work He will give us to do."

The constant reminders of past input and some very poignant messages finally caused me to keep a journal. Am I ever glad I did! What a source of encouragement those words have been through the years. Just as God reminded the Israelites to keep rehearsing the events of their national history, so it is good to learn to do the same for ourselves; and to teach our children of our Father's wonderful workings that happen right here and now. Moses was not only instructed to write the early history, but also to teach the nation the song of their salvation. That is good for us to do, too. Sing your family's history and inject some Alleluias. Singing puts it in your memory forever. Where did Madison Avenue learn to use music to teach and push us to new products? From the Bible! (Don't tell; they will deny it!)

I'm sure we are not the first family to have more than one gigantic hurdle to overcome. So why write about it? First of all we want to give God the glory for the many marvelous things He has done. Things we could never have imagined or anticipated and that came so differently for each child. Some came as unwanted changes. We did not know what lay ahead that would so dramatically and defiantly alter our lives. We weren't asked and we weren't consulted. Robert's future plans seemed so straightforward; we saw an impassioned future. His desires and longings could only be seen by us as God's plan. But there arose a great contradiction and we were not there to help. Yet God's way is perfect. There is so much to wonder about our Heavenly Father, but then we've got forever to see His power, strength, and love. To experience His peace is to be participating in the treasure and wealth of the dark and secret places promised in Isaiah 45:3. Also, it is good to encourage one another to be alert to the needs of those who struggle—the deaf, the blind, the lame, and the poor. In so doing there are also the manifold blessings that boomerang to us.

You will also find examples as you watch our daughter, a person who never had "special needs" until calamity targeted our family, as she reaches out in real concern and caring compassion to other people with special needs. You will see her encourage anyone who crosses her path and what happens so many times is "marvelous in our eyes." It is surely the Love of Jesus that He generously imparts to her. With both of our children, God required of us a great letting go as in; "Let be, and know that I am God" (Psalm 46:10 AMP).

As I continued journaling sometimes I was writing prayers, at other times poetry or just writing thoughts as they came to me. Much of what you'll read is taken directly from my notes, important lessons to me that may, with God's direction, be helpful to others. At one time I was sketching and meditating as God impressed on me certain scriptures. I was sitting with Shiona for long weeks after she came home from an extended hospital stay, just needing to be near her and to have a quiet occupation for my fingers. Looking back, this was a very precious yet anxious time, but I was being comforted and so was Shiona. It has become for me one of the "blessings in the bundle," as I call it. The results of this time are the pen and ink drawings that introduce each chapter. I refer to them as "Windows on the Word."

If there is a blessing for others in this book, let God be praised. The story is His. It could never have been planned by us, and we would not have chosen His way if He had told us or asked our permission. He has been the Guide and will be even to the end. It all happened and only He knew and knows where and to whom this story will go. As Corrie said so well, "Experiences and memories are the mysterious and perfect preparation for the work He will give us to do."

The Lord will perfect that which concerns me; Your mercy and loving-kindness, O Lord, endure forever— forsake not the works of Your own hands. (Psalm 138:8 AMP)

Now it is time for you to . . .

. . . . MEET THE MUTHMANNS

Jay and I met at Covenant College in St. Louis. The new St. Louis campus opened for the fall term in 1956. There would be a few new foreign students, one from Germany. Yeah, I'd like to meet him; my father's background was German. *Could be interesting*, I thought. I arrived from California where I had spent the last two years at Covenant while it was located in Pasadena. A new year, a fresh start appealed to me. Before Christmas break, Juergen (his German name) and I were dating. I was learning about his German family. His dad was a pastor in the Reformed Church in West Germany, his mother helped in the congregation. There was a lot of history to learn about his family, since they had lived through the Nazi turmoil.

Juergen was very thankful to be able to fulfill his child-hood dream of coming to the United States. That dream began with his acquaintance with Dr. Robert G. Rayburn (founding president of Covenant College) since his duties as a chaplain in the United States army made it logical that he would meet his counterpart, local German pastor, Dr. Erich Muthmann, who was Jay's father. So Jay came with attachments, not exactly an unknown. While the college was still located in Pasadena, my family and our home became a home away from home for many students. My mother and I cooked many meals during a difficult transition period for Covenant students while arrangements were being made for the total college to relocate and become officially Covenant College.

Spring 1957 was the year I graduated. Jay still had several years to finish, but he decided it would be "educational" to spend the summer in California, besides the added incentive to keep seeing Janet! He returned to St. Louis in the fall, came back to California in December, and we were married in my parents lovely home on January 3, 1958.

We made Pasadena our home for the next ten years. Besides his job, Jay also found time to study and finish his degree. During this time we welcomed our first born, Robert in 1959, and Shiona in 1963. Jay's parents arrived from Germany for a winter visit in Southern California. It was a wonderful opportunity for them to meet their daughter-in-law and their first grandson, and likewise for me to be introduced to Mutti and Vati, and for Robert to meet another set of grandparents. This get-together incited me to get to know them better, and to see Jay's homeland. I also felt that ten years was a long time for someone to keep extending his visa and not going home for a visit. So after talking about this seriously, Jay took a leave of absence from his work, we sold our home, stored our possessions, and took off for a summer in Germany. Shiona was three and Robert was seven. They were old enough and four months was long enough to absorb the new and the different people, friends, land, and language. This opportunity to spend time in Jay's homeland made for great occasions to celebrate. We could finally share together.

During this summer visit, Omi supervised the "Peanuts Gang" (our children and the village children) in the backyard play area. She was especially tuned in to children and we always heard all about the escapades in the evening. Opi spent meaningful time with our children in his own special way. He was soon convinced of and impressed by their childlike faith in Jesus, and asked our permission to baptize them by sprinkling on a Sunday morning in his church. Our children had been dedicated to the Lord in our own living room a few years earlier since our differences in Christian upbringing meant we would compromise on various things, baptism being one of those. We agreed with all our hearts and Opi also used the occasion to talk about "believer's baptism." In the Reformed Faith infant sprinkling is normal. It was also nearing his retirement, so altogether it became a great time of celebration for the family. Such is our Heavenly Father!

Before we left Germany at the end of summer, we took a special detour while on an excursion to visit one of several German factories that General Electric was implementing in various parts of Europe. Jay had the opportunity to talk to the president of this operation and asked about the possibility of a transfer. He was encouraged to follow through on our return home.

When we arrived back in California, we were all surprised that Jay was offered a transfer to Portland, Oregon, which he gladly accepted; an unanticipated opportunity to live away from the smoggy southland. It wasn't long until he started talking to his new boss about the possibility of the transfer to Germany. Two and a half years of enjoying Portland and surrounding areas, the order finally came that our family would be Germany dwellers. It was quite an excitement for us, but caused a bit of anguish for my parents. We would miss them, and we would miss the beautiful northwest, though we knew we would be back to the states again. The company took care of all our household, and were pleased to get a German speaking employee for the situations they were anticipating overseas.

As we settled ourselves in Kassel, Robert, Shiona and I continued our German lessons and practiced on the neighbors, the store-keepers, the school teachers, and sometimes a tutor. By now, Robert was almost ten and Shiona was almost six; so off to school they went. Robert didn't like being called "Ami" (slang for American), since he held a valid German citizenship through his dad. His German grandfather had seen to that on our earlier visit, so why didn't his school friends accept it? It remained an unanswered question, but didn't spoil the friendships he was making. Shiona, brave little girl, caught hold of the hand of the frightened little German boy upstairs and helped him get used to going to school! They also became very good friends. We met many young United States military people. Hardly a weekend went by that our dining room table wasn't surrounded by these new friends. Music and games, and much conversation occupied the afternoon and evening and our kids happily joined in.

These few paragraphs capture rather quickly the earliest years. As he grew, Robert's interests lay in the direction of the geo-political make-up of the world, next came agriculture, and horticulture. There were always many side interests such as music, youth group, and other teen interests. For Robert, our prayers were for a deepening interest in the Bible, thinking mostly of the Old Testament history and development of ancient Israel, and God's omnipotent hand in the affairs of men. This awareness would be well-served when coupled with his strong interest in current world affairs. Shiona was always the people lover, the singer, the dancer, the entertainer. You will read more about these interest areas, and most of all how Jesus and His Father hovered over and around us in our family life.

These were the young years; children growing, moving often with Jay's job changes, and learning to pray about everything. Then searching the Word as bumps and twisting turns came along as they do for all God's people. But God was there as He always is, guiding, teaching, urging us to trust and obey. In the pages that follow you will get to know us better. Some parts are narrative, and because we are real people, you will "hear" us talking. Other parts are significant showing how our Father was teaching us. As we all find when He gives us work to do, we struggle, we agonize, but our eyes are opened more and more while we are learning that, "greater is He who is in you than he who is in the world" (1 John 4:4).

As the earth brings forth its sprouts, and as a garden causes the things sown in it to spring up, so the LORD GOD will cause righteousness and praise to spring up before all the nations. Isaiah 61:11

Chapter Two

In His Garden

In His Garden

A tight closed bud
Of secret hue
Does no aroma shed;

Till turned toward light,
Through rain and wind,
It lifts a full-blown head.

With fragrant beauty
Let me so bloom
And grace Thy flower bed.

All my springs of joy are from Thee. (Psalm 87:7 KJV)
Make my garden breathe out fragrance.
(Song of Solomon 4:16)

*   *   *   *   *

Summertime Ballet

With one hundred degree heat, I gave up on the Resurrection Lilies I had been looking forward to. What a sad feeling. Expecting to see my ballerinas in pink, I was sure they would not show up in those lovely pink dresses dancing from one side of my garden to the other. Oh no, they were not in straight rows. They were gathered here and there in clumps of seven to ten bulbs each. If they came up as expected there would be that many stems with up to six ladies on each stem. It had been a beautiful spring, good weather for planting, but when summer came, it came on so hot!

Finally one Sunday, after many days of record heat, we looked up to cloudy skies. The bright blue was gone and it didn't take long until the winds whipped up to sixty miles an hour. First came the rain, one and a half inches in one and a half hours, then hail and a very forbidding sky. We sat out the darkness hoping there would be no tornado warnings. We stayed away from windows willing the trees to "please sway with the wind and don't damage roofs." Monday came, a perfect day, a day to finish planting a small remaining purchase of "must haves." Then I looked around the garden barely thinking that maybe, just maybe, the lilies decided to arise. "Surprise Lilies," they are sometimes called, and yes, there to my surprise they did decide to arise; up to eight inches in twenty-four hours!

I stood there gaping, "Is this for real?"

I looked to all the places where I had planted my dancing ladies, and yes, they were coming, some slower than others, but coming on stage, getting ready for the Summertime Ballet. In two more days or so the show would begin; pink ballerinas across my garden!

Singing in my heart were the words from Psalm 68:1, "Let God arise and His enemies be scattered, let God arise and His enemies be scattered; Let God, Let God arise!" I thought, *God will arise out of any heap of trouble. He will arise with comfort, with a refreshing well of water, with a touch on a life, with health and healing, guidance and peace.* I also remember it says, "He will come suddenly to His temple" (Malachi 3:1). We are His temple. He lives with us and in us by His Holy Spirit. God will never leave us nor forsake us; He will never leave us comfortless! What I had just witnessed in the sudden arrival of my lilies was a beautiful demonstration of how God loves and cares for us. So excited about my dancing ladies in pink, I did the math and came up with a ballet company of at least fifteen hundred dancers! Wow!

The summer drought had discouraged my lilies. But like the woman at the well (John 4) who needed a deep, ever-lasting drink, the lilies came up smiling after the rain just as that thirsty woman hurried to spread her Good News of Living Water.

Therefore, you will joyously draw water from the springs of salvation. And, in that day, you will say, "Give thanks to the Lord! Call on His Name, make known His deeds among the peoples; make them remember that His Name is exalted." (Isaiah 12:3-4)

We can come up smiling, too, when there has been a dry season in our life. God will never say, "No!" to those He loves. He says, "Let the one who is thirsty come; let the one who wishes take the water of life without cost " (Revelation 22:17). Like the lilies without water would be dead; where would we be without the Water of Life?

*   *   *   *   *

Refreshing

Let not these leaves droop down.
Sometimes this soil seems so parched;
Yet Your mercies, Your kindness,
Your love, are new every morning.

And You remind me again;
"How welcome is the morning light!
How refreshing the early dew!
Restoring the wasteland of yesterdays,
Renewing again dry stubborn soil."

With eyes toward the Savior,
With arms outstretched,
With my heart crying out, I plead,
"Freshen this drooping soul again."

Then, like a gentle soft rain
On newly mown grass
Comes a strong lifting up
On the Everlasting Arms.

Let now the beauty of our Lord be upon us. (Psalm 90:17)

Though the fig tree should not blossom, and there be no fruit on the vines, though the yield of the olive fail, and the fields produce no food, though the flocks should be cut off from the fold and there be no cattle in the stalls. Yet will I exult in the Lord I will rejoice in the God of my salvation GOD the LORD is my STRENGTH Hab.3.17.19

Chapter Three

A Cold Wintry Day

Broken and Fragmented

At some moment in our awakening we begin to learn about brokenness. A few basic facts: *We were born into a broken world, which means we are all broken.* But, You, Lord, were broken to redeem us. Yes, we are all broken, born broken: In Him we are made whole. Made whole for what? To be broken again? Yes, broken again—for His purpose, His glory. He is breaking us away from our selfishness, our wish to be noticed, and to be important perhaps. He knows better than we how our thoughts and desires can carry us far away from His purposes.

We may be broken again and again as God works in us, preparing us for His plan, His purpose, His glory, and His usefulness. Or simply getting our attention! Unaware of what the future holds; we can be the more amazed in our thankfulness as He gives us a glimpse and surprise from time to time.

Brokenness is not wasted in God's accounting. God excels in working with brokenness. Remember the pitchers, when broken; the sudden light routed the enemy! (Judges 7:16-21). Remember the alabaster box, broken for the anointing! (Mark 14:3). Recall the broken bread, the hungry

To feed! (Matthew 14:19). And finally Jesus was broken, us to redeem! In our Lord's eyes nothing is wasted. Notice Peter's brokenness, his denial of Jesus. How that speaks to us! Ashamed to say "Jesus" when speaking to someone? Think also for a moment of Peter's cry, "Help me, Lord, I'm sinking" (Matthew 14:31). What happened there? Oh, that's it, not good to take our eyes off Jesus!

It is comforting to think of these Words of Jesus, "Gather up the fragments that nothing be lost" (John 6:13). Our world is a broken and fragmented world since Adam and Eve. If Jesus has broken us, and we take a look with Him at our life, don't we see a handful of fragments after the breaking? Is He waiting for us to humbly hand Him the fragments along with our answer, "Yes, Lord, Your will be done" (Luke 5:32)? Jesus knew, more than we can even think, of the brokenness that made critical His plan for redemption.

It was toward the end of the day, after the crowd sat down and had been fed, that Jesus said to His disciples, "Gather up all the fragments that nothing be lost." No thought of waste, only of usefulness. Fragments are broken pieces, even leftovers. In God's hands these broken pieces and scraps become the material for new beginnings, new beauty, and new usefulness. My thought is that this applies to all of our life. Nothing is waste, nothing will be lost, and all will be accounted for and used for His glory. He brings all things, even the smallest bits, together for good!

The more years that pass by, the more remarkable it seems. At the end of a difficult day, I seem to be offering Him bits and pieces. Humbly handing Him snips and shreds, and as in the miracle, He knows what to do with them. Someday, when all the leftovers are gathered up, I'm convinced the beauty of Jesus will shine through everything we offered Him that to us were the scraps off the workroom floor. He will display to us beauty much greater than the prize quilt made from the years of gathering the fragments off the seamstress' sewing room floor.

> *Bits and pieces*
> *Mere fragments of life;*
> *But all joined together*
> *Show the beauty of Christ.*

When God adjusts our perspective and we recognize that our Father is in every detail of our lives, we begin to see the only way is to yield; that it is He who is:

Breaking us,
   Shaking us,
      Disturbing us,
         Emptying us.

Only then do we search with all our being for Him, and we cry out, "Are You in this with me?" We then run with all our might to the Strong Tower, to the place where His Presence dwells. I believe we often won't go there until we are encouraged—urged to go when we run out of our own strength and feeble resources. How hard it is to let go. How easy it is to fall back on that old way, "I can do this by myself." We long to know Him, but how we hesitate to pay the price, and there are no bargain prices. He is not interested in our things or our stuff. He is interested in us. He wants to first of all make us all new. When you think of it our resources, compared to the riches in Christ Jesus which the Father says belong to us, are only useless substitutes that we frantically hoard. We cannot offer God our goodness, our accomplishments or our righteousness. No, we are poor, blind, and naked. There is only this life in which to take the offer to buy the field and own the Treasure. Take all that

He hands you and embrace it; He will unfold His love, His goodness, and His mercy in manifold ways.

For thus says the High exalted One, who lives forever, whose name is Holy. . . "I dwell in the high and holy place and also with the contrite and lowly of spirit." (Isaiah 57:15)

I thought about Ruth, the Moabitess, a gleaner in Judea. A widow, a stranger, a foreigner, who followed the harvesters doing the only thing she could to help her mother-in-law, Naomi. Yes, she lived for years as a foreigner in Moab. Both Ruth and Naomi lost husbands and Naomi lost sons, too. Naomi said to Ruth, "I'm nothing, with nothing to give. I can't help you, Ruth. Go home to your parents. I must go back to Judea." Ruth responds, "I also am nothing, but I want to go with you. You have God; I want to have a share in what is left of your life." So Naomi shared her fragmented life; just fragments of a broken life (Ruth 1:6-18 and following).

For who has despised the day of small things? (Zechariah 4:10)

In Israel, Ruth gleaned fragments of barley left in the fields after the harvesters. Naomi prepared them so together they could eat. God watched and God blessed the fragments. Ruth was learning to trust and Naomi was being restored. Multiplied blessings followed. Boaz found Ruth gathering in his fields. Surely the Lord went with her, following behind, and going before, as she gathered the leftovers. The Lord had plans for her, "plans for good and not evil to give her a future and a hope" (Jeremiah 29:11). These were secret plans that Ruth didn't know, for as she was gathering the remnants of barley, God was gathering together the remnants and brokenness of her life. Plans so that she would no longer be an outsider.

Ruth had a kinsman redeemer and I can hear her asking, "My mother, what did you say? A kinsman redeemer? Whatever is that?" Naomi told Ruth that Boaz was her closest relative and could marry her and redeem to her all of what was her husband's. Ruth was beginning to learn about the Lord God of Israel. Her new life was just starting to happen. Looking into the future we learn Ruth would be the mother of Obed, the grandmother of Jesse, great-grandmother of King David, (the singing shepherd). And, she would be mentioned in the lineage of Jesus—King Jesus!

How wonderful is our Lord! In His family there are no outsiders, none so inconspicuous that place cannot be found for them. How beautifully He gathered up the fragments of her life, planning for her when she was not aware. God draws us in, and gathers up all the loose threads and torn pieces. Looking up to Him we can hear Him say, "Quiet, dear, I'll gather up all the pieces, broken and torn, and nothing will be lost." Yes, He will make something lovely out of it all! The loveliness of Christ in each of us! He will rejoice over us with shouts of joy!

Redeem! Redeem!
Gather the fragments!
Let nothing be lost!

Did Ruth and Boaz see the whole picture? No, and we also will not see the whole picture of what God has planned for us when we yield to Him, saying, "Your will be done." Follow on down the line to Joseph and Mary who, by the Holy Spirit, gave birth to the Son of God.

Behold, the virgin shall be with child, and shall bear a Son, and they shall call His name Immanuel. . .God with us. And you shall call His name Jesus. (Matthew 1:23, 21)

This Jesus is our Kinsman Redeemer! He humbled Himself and took on our humanity in order to become the sacrifice for our sins. He bought us with His blood.

Not my will, but Thy will be done. (Luke 22:42)

Delay may try to undermine our trust, but we can't listen to the lie that says, "You are forgotten." Jesus has overcome all things, and He will never leave us nor forsake us. In the time of waiting, read this:

Therefore the Lord longs (waits) to be gracious to you, and therefore He waits on high to have compassion on you. For the Lord is a God of justice. How blessed are all those who long (wait) for Him. (Isaiah 30:18)

* * * * *

Sorrow Met by Joy

A solemn joy - Yes, I have known this.
His love underscored in a profound way:
Death without the sting
Beauty out of ashes
Springs in the desert
Life in a weary land.
Today I know a solemn joy, by faith I understand,
Then 'twill be pure joy: a joy of the purest sound.
It comes with the words He said, "I have overcome the world" (John 16:33).
On this I take my stand. "Take joy," says the Lamb.

38

Robert Reid, our son and first-born, came to us with a zest for living and intense curiosity that stayed with him throughout his life. His arrival was an early sign of spring so we called him Robin, until kindergarten, when his rightful name appealed to him more. When he was four years old he was proud to become a big brother to his sister Shiona. His excitement and anticipation at having a new playmate met with a little disappointment when he realized she needed time to begin to appreciate his cars and trucks. However, he eagerly introduced her to anyone who would stop and listen as he explained her Irish-Gaelic name for Janet, and that she was born on his mother's birthday.

We were a happy family of four, and since Papa was born in Germany, there surfaced a great desire to experience Germany as a family. A four-month visit the summer of 1966 was just the beginning. We stayed with the grandparents in a little known part of Germany that had a long history of being passed back and forth between Germany and Holland. Our feet were in Germany but Holland was at our finger tips. Holland seemed more Christian than Germany, and it was not unusual that Opi, who was the pastor, had to visit the Dutch Baroness to ensure that his theology was truly of the reformed faith before being approved for the church he was to shepherd.

Holland was also noteworthy for being child friendly, so it was very pleasant to be living in Lage, a small village on the Dutch border. I remember one day when we were crossing the border into Holland, the border patrol, seeing on my passport I was from United States, greeted me with, "See you later, alligator." It startled me, but I managed to speak, "After a while, crocodile," and we had a good laugh! We spent many happy days during that visit to Omi and Opi.

Two years after our visit, Jay received an invitation to be part of a GE plan to implement factories in Germany. For the next three years we lived in Germany, three of us learning the language, getting well-acquainted with relatives, and digesting German life. It was an exciting time for all of us. During those three years Robert and Shiona went to German schools. It was a striking moment for Robert when the United States sent astronauts to the moon.

But at school his religions teacher mocked God by saying, "There couldn't be a Jesus or heaven because the astronauts didn't see either when they were in outer space."

She concluded to the class that this obviously put these stories and any other Bible stories in the area of legend.

"Now," she said, "there isn't anyone in this class that believes there is a God, is there?" End of subject.

But Robert stood up to respond saying, "I know God is alive because He lives in my heart!"

Thereupon he was told to stay after school for some discussion about Christianity in America!

Later that day his teacher said to him, "You are American, Robert, and I realize a lot of Americans still believe those things, but I admire you for your faith and being able to stand up and say it. That's all, Robert."

We came home to America as though we just finished a three-year course of German, university style! Robert excelled in German and as soon as he got into high school he was asked to substitute for the German teacher. That was a challenge he was very excited to accept. He had his own cubicle in the teachers' room and was given a list of books from which he could order reading material to keep up his German. As a ninth-grade student-teacher, he enjoyed it. I would have loved to peek in the room, but didn't dare. I took his word for it that he could keep control of the class, since many were his friends!

Beginning his senior year, he felt strongly that the Lord wanted him in the high school that was an extension of our Church. He had worked hard at being elected Senior Class president, and his dad wondered at this sudden upheaval.

This would be an enormous change, but I can still hear the words that spoke resolve, "Listen, Dad, when God tells you to do something, you better do it."

He presented his arguments to his Dad who listened and offered some foreseeable difficulties, such as wearing a uniform and keeping his hair above the collar. But Robert's desire prevailed and he followed what he believed God wanted. Later, all our concerns about his school change in his senior year vanished in light of the events that ensued.

While we were living in Germany Shiona sustained a serious head injury followed by epilepsy. The accident happened in our apartment when she climbed on a chair while reaching to the top of the piano. The chair slipped and not able to break the fall with her hands, her forehead struck the floor full force. She was unconscious for some moments. We had no immediate concerns about long lasting complications while she was in grade school and medications controlled the seizures quite well. So life continued on with the children acclimating to life in the Pacific Northwest, a wonderful place to live in the 1970's.

Soon we got glimpses of change coming over the horizon. Robert was now in his first year of Bible College, and Shiona started high school. I had been teaching kindergarten for the last couple of years. Then Jay was offered a position in the Poughkeepsie, New York office that would mean less travel. That appealed to us, even though Jay's traveling in the northwest, meant we could all enjoy his trips to Northern California during the summer. But now we faced the big challenge of separation, since Robert would be staying in Oregon at the Bible College. Moving away from the familiar, from Robert, and our friends in Portland, and grandparents in California would not be easy. Nevertheless, Robert and Shiona encouraged the move. The decision was made, and Robert arranged to live at home, instead of staying in the dorms, while Jay began his new job in New York. Shiona and I enjoyed having Robert ("Bob" at this time in his life) at home with us until we moved.

It was during this time that Bob showed me two drawings, pencil sketches, that he said came to him during times of prayer. One was a picture of a potted plant, as if groaning and struggling with roots coming out of the bottom of the cracked pot.

He asked me what I saw in the picture and I responded with, "Looks like it needs a new home—a new planting or transplanting."

The other picture was of a broken candle that was still lit, illuminating the surrounding area. He asked the same question and I asked him what he thought it meant. We were both puzzled. It just seemed an odd concept. Sometime later both of these took on a good deal of meaning. It was not unusual for us to be shown bits and pieces of sketches, since Bob had been doodling and drawing ever since he could hold a pencil.

March came. Soon it would be time to say *goodbye* to Oregon. Jay had picked out the house for us in the small town of Hopewell Junction and came back with pictures, and for last minute business. Our last evening together was very special. One particular highlight was the prayer that Bob offered, asking God "for deepening relationships that would mean strong memories for the times coming, when we must rely on the relationships that have been formed in the past, because we won't always have each other's presence any time we want it."

I felt immediately that I had to write this down, and left the room. I needed to remember very carefully Bob's prayer. His expression blessed me, and I felt God was in this. God's knowing and caring saturated the awareness of His presence that evening. The coming changes would be difficult and so much seemed backward. Isn't it the children who leave home? Bob's plans and ideas were coming quickly: a very special friend, and his very special desires for the future. I think each of us were experiencing trembling hearts on that last evening together.

Early in May we made the big move. Shiona and I had to learn all about Hopewell Junction; find her new school, the stores that would be new to us, the people at the Fellowship we planned to associate with, and make some new friends. There were a few weeks of school for Shiona before the summer break, giving her a chance to make a few friends to help fill the summer months. On our last days with Bob, he told of his plan to visit us in early summer. But not many weeks later he had to inform us that his plans had changed. His summer employment was interfering because of a strike, and he promised to keep the garden center in the store open, even though it would require very long hours and postpone his trip to the end of summer, if that would be possible. Happily a phone call in early July informed us that he would be able to fly to New York near the end of the month. He calculated that we would have ten wonderful days together before he would start his second year at Portland Bible College. This two year curriculum Jay asked Bob to do before going to university.

Meanwhile, Shiona was making friends in the neighborhood, and learning about the surrounding areas, among which was a small lake for swimming with friends. She heard all about John Jay high school, and she did a lot of talking about her big brother, Bob, whom they all wanted to meet.

Finally, the anticipated visit became a reality. Ten whole days together offered family trips, so we drove to everyplace we thought would be of interest to him. Our pastor arranged a trip to the United Nations building where Bob, because he began translating for some German tourists, was offered a job in the translation department if he would like to come back to New York! Of course, he was delighted to think that the three years in German schools were worthwhile. But I could hardly think that busy New York City would be a place that would attract him to work and live.

Ten days went by too fast. The morning Bob left for Oregon, Jay was also leaving for Canada. We said the hard-to-say good-byes, hugged and thanked Bob for coming into our family, and the many happy years we had together.

He answered, "Oh, Mom, I didn't have anything to do with it, and it hasn't been all good."

But to me it had been, even though there were a couple of troubling teen years, which our Father had graciously led us through. Now Bob was leaving us, just as I thought it should be. Again he promised to be back. The limo came for Jay, but Bob caught it before it left the driveway and had another good-bye with his Dad.

With all that is put into a family, the love, caring, sharing of triumphs and tragedies, the good times and the other times, between the four of us we had a relationship of love, respect, forgiveness, and the need of the moment enabled each of us to express the deepest feelings of our hearts. On his next birthday, Bob would be twenty and approaching the end of his second year in college. We spent many hours during his visit talking over the immediate years ahead and the possibilities they held for him.

Anticipating various circumstantial changes, our hearts were responding in expressions of love and gratitude. Jay dispensed many words of wisdom that Bob promised to heed. We expected to face and embrace the changes that these next years would unfold. We all knew that our special, unique family of four would most likely be altered in some way. One of Bob's dreams was an extended visit behind the Iron Curtain. We tried to realistically approach even this separation, and saw the present separation as practice for all of us.

Shiona and I had the privilege of driving Bob to the place where the limo would take him to Kennedy airport. Too quickly it was girl time for Shiona and me. Suddenly we had plenty of time to think and talk about our visit with Bob. She and Bob had a special big brother-little sister relationship, and she began sharing some of their secrets with me. Nevertheless, it was a long day after the excitement of ten days being together. Bob called us that evening after his flight and we recounted our special week and the particular joys of the visit. Jay would be back from Canada the next day.

Eight o'clock Thursday evening finally came. Shiona and I would have been at church except that Jay had specifically asked us to stay home and have a late dinner with him.

As he walked in the door the phone was ringing. I picked it up.

"Hello," I answered.

"Janet, is your husband at home? This is Pastor Iverson in Portland."

"Oh, my goodness, why yes, he is. In fact he just came in the door. Hold on."

Jay took the phone and went into the bedroom. Looking at his face, Shiona and I knew that something was wrong.

He put the phone down, slightly lifting his head as he stood up and said slowly, his voice weak and heavy, "Robert, our Robert. Oh, Janet, our son. He's gone, he went to be with Jesus."

Instantly we were hugging each other, holding on, reaching for strength.

Then Shiona started saying, "We have to hold on to Jesus. Robert is with Jesus, Robert is with Jesus."

We were in shock. Robert was just nineteen, and Shiona, little sister, was fifteen. We were in a new place, far away from family and friends, new in our church fellowship and in our neighborhood. Who can instantly grasp the unwanted news? We looked to Jesus. We cried, we prayed, we hurt, we tried to sleep, it was fitful, and for myself, I found no sleep. We didn't want this.

It was by the Lord's great love and mercy that we had just spent those last ten days with Robert. We were reliving all the years of family fun, the travels, and so many special memories. Then he flew back to Oregon to begin classes. The second day after his arrival, he and his good friend went to the Clackamas River for their annual swim. Robert, good swimmer though he was, didn't make it across. Jesus took him out of the river and brought him Home. Later, a friend wrote to us, giving us this scripture, "He sent from on high, He took me; He drew me out of many waters" (Psalm 18:16). We felt this is what Bob would say, could he tell us. Shiona and I recalled reading together that same morning Psalm 16. It held many comforting words for us.

Thou wilt make known to me the path of life; in Thy presence is fullness of joy, in Thy right hand there are pleasures forevermore; the lines have fallen to me in pleasant places.

We were to recall these scriptures and many more in the days to come. Through these verses and in other ways, God began to comfort each of us. For myself, the Lord provided His own way of communicating with me by a song in the night. The song began when I lay down and did not stop until I got up early the next morning having never slept.

The song, by Dick and Melody Tunney, was this:

There is joy, joy, joy in the House of the Lord
And a time of singing.
There is joy, joy, joy in the House of the Lord
And praises ringing.
For the winter is over past and gone,
Jesus wiped all my tears away.
There is joy, joy, joy in the House of the lord
And a brand new Day.

Certainly it is a song for rejoicing, but right then I could not rejoice. I couldn't grasp the joy. But at the same time I truly believed that Robert was rejoicing, and I would never want to take that away from him, nor could I. He was ready to be with Jesus, but this early in life? The promise to rejoice for him was waiting for me. But in these days of grief, days when I couldn't look passed that day, I didn't understand why God had taken him away from us. I kept thinking, this song is not for me, but on and on it played in my mind and spirit.

Then one day I found four words which explained this unusual singing inside me. It was the time of restoration and great temple worship in 2 Chronicles, "And the song sang. . ." (2 Chronicles 29:28). God in His love for me sent a song, like He would send an angel, to comfort me. It was comfort I needed at this very significant moment of getting things straight. Robert belonged to Him, he had been on loan to us. Our time for meaningful input in his life was over. This was indeed a brand new day, not just for Robert, but also for his parents and his sister.

Then my thoughts would go back to, "after all his life was just beginning" or so I thought. He had plans; he was to get married next summer. He was looking forward to going to Eastern Europe to work with a pastor friend in Yugoslavia. No, No, No, I tried to refuse it all. I could find all kinds of reasons not to be lifted to joy at this moment. But God would wait for me. Yes, wait for me to let go and find joy in His doings. We see so much for our children, our loved ones, and God waits, slowly pouring in the oil for our healing, from friends who simply hold us in their arms. God does send them, not with exhortation, but by reading a psalm or two and a quiet prayer, and yes, a cup of tea, just sitting together, holding a hand. Comfort comes as He sends it.

There is truth in this hymn of Anna B. Russell from long ago. It speaks of implanted songs:

There is never a day so dreary,
There is never a night so long,
But the soul that is trusting Jesus,
Will somewhere find a song.
Wonderful, wonderful Jesus,
In the heart He implanteth a song:
A song of deliverance,
Of courage, of strength;
In the heart He implanteth a song.

I truly believe that God does implant songs in our hearts by the Holy Spirit. How He loves us!

We were on the plane taking us to Portland for the Memorial Service. I had in my hand a notebook where I kept special memories. I began reading what I had written just two weeks before Bob's visit. As I read I was reminded of those intimate moments with my Savior. I had been reading about Mary and her alabaster box of precious ointment.

Reflecting on that, Jesus seemed to be asking me, "What do you offer Me, that is most precious to you?"

I answered, "My family, Jay, Bob, and Shiona. They are Yours, Lord. Use them, take them as You will."

I felt the tears come. I reached for my journal and wrote it all down, not to forget those poignant moments sitting in His presence, laying my treasures that He had given me on the altar —giving them to Jesus. Little did I know, but God knew that our family would be further scattered. Reflecting on that act before the Lord, I have been in awe many hundreds of times. How thankful I am that I said, "Yes" to the Lord. I was still bewildered that such a conversation took place. Yet, unknown to me, my Father had placed this preparation in my heart. He knew, but I did not know. But right then on the way to Portland, my heart was breaking. I remembered that day and the prayer of relinquishment. I had given Robert to Jesus.

Only a few days after the Memorial Service, I opened Robert's journal and read these words, "I know He wants my life and I have given my life to Him for any purpose that would be to His benefit." It goes without saying that this was indeed a solemn kind of comfort.

I sat back with his journal in my hands, thinking about a November day in 1963. It was Sunday morning. Jay was at church teaching young boys. Robin (his pre-school nickname) and I were at home with baby Shiona. Over the radio came the flash news that President Kennedy had been assassinated.

Then came the questions from my four-year old, "Mommy, what does that mean? Where is he now? What about Grandma, and Grandpa? If they died where would they be?"

We talked and he listened, this time with both ears. He had nothing else on his mind. For several days Robin was pre-occupied with this thought of dying and the implications that his young mind could comprehend and grapple with. He would sit thinking for some moments then speak his next concern. He wanted to be sure that loving Jesus meant what I said about being with Jesus in Heaven when we have asked Him into our hearts. We talked about Jesus dying on the cross, why it was necessary.

Jesus died for our sins, for all the wrong things we had done, I told him and then I asked, "Do you know what that means, Robin?"

A few more questions and then together we knelt by the chair and he asked Jesus into his heart. So now sitting, reading what he said in his own words about his own giving of himself to his Savior, my heart had to feel more at ease. I realized it was my giving of him; he had already given himself wholly to Jesus. Perhaps a little of the letting go was taking place even now.

Recently, in reading a page from C. L. Spurgeon's *The Treasury of David*, I saw the clear connection. Quoting

Spurgeon, "Oh, I am sure, though it were agony, you would start from your feet, and say, 'Jesus, not my will, but Thine be done.' You would give up your prayer for your loved one's life, if you could realize the thoughts that Christ is praying in the opposite direction - *'Father, I will that they also, whom Thou hast given Me, be with Me where I am'* (John 17:24). 'Lord, Thou shalt have them.' By faith we let them go." Like Abraham and King David we shall have them again, by faith in the New Earth and even now as we worship in faith believing that all His children are before Him. *Thank You, Father.*

In trials, sorrow and joy have met because of Jesus. He won that place for us so we always have the joy before us, even in sorrow. It will be beyond us for a season. But He bids us to follow Him and says, "Behold I make all things new" (Revelation 21:5). "Let us run with endurance the race that is set before us, fixing our eyes on Jesus the author and perfecter of faith, who for the joy set before Him endured the cross" (Hebrews 12:1-2). Because He endured the cross, and with this joy that He gave us, which for a time is shrouded in darkness, can we not endure the sorrow that comes in our life? This joy is one gift among the promises of Isaiah 45:2-3.

I will go before you and make the rough places smooth. . . . And I will give you the treasures of darkness, and hidden wealth of secret places, in order that you may know that it is I, the Lord, the God of Israel, who calls you by your name.

* * * * *

At the top of the painting you see the mountain with the castle-like city coming down over the clouds. The old sun, the sea and old earth in lower left corner are receding. All things are to become new.

Postcard from Heaven

In our sorrowful trip to Portland, we had to do the necessary thing of folding up Robert's dorm life. We traveled out with a couple of empty suitcases to help in the relocation of his possessions. Without him this would be difficult indeed. Much was given to his friends, but we rolled up a large canvas, an oil painting he had painted a year or so before. We remembered his surprise at being awarded third place in the Gladstone, Oregon Art Show, since it was the first time he had ever entered an art show.

When we got back home I took it to the art and frame shop in a small town nearby, and left anxious to return for it in a few days. It wasn't long until I was on my way back to pick it up. The shop owner brought it out, uncovered it and there it was: *The Postcard from Heaven*, from Robert. This is the scripture that he chose to display with his painting:

> *And I saw a new heaven and a new earth; for the first heaven and the first earth were passed away; and there was no more sea. And I, John, saw the holy city, new Jerusalem, coming down from God out of heaven, prepared as a bride adorned for her husband. And I heard a great voice out of heaven saying, "Behold the tabernacle of God is with men, and He will dwell with them, and they shall be His people, and God himself shall be with them, and be their God. And God shall wipe away all tears from their eyes; and there shall be no more death, neither sorrow, nor crying, neither shall there be any more pain: for the former things are passed away.* (Revelation 21:1-4)

At the top of the painting is the mountain of the Lord with the Holy City on top coming down above clouds of glory, above the receding sea, the sun and the old earth. "All things are being made new" is the message in the painting. If our discomfort in grief can be comforted, only God can do it. This painting was planned in Robert's mind, but its purpose was in God's plan. For us, it has been comfort indeed!

This was surely an opportunity to unravel back to Robert's high school days and the gladness God had given us in our son. Now even a Postcard from his new Home. Admittedly we looked at the painting with eyes wet with tears, but the rainbow promise was in our hearts. Today it still maintains a prominent place in our home, a constant reminder that a Great Reunion lies ahead.

*   *   *   *   *

If Thy law had not been my delight, then I would have perished in my affliction. (Psalm 119:92)

The darkest days of our lives were now upon us. Robert was no longer with us; our families were in California and Germany; close friends were in Oregon and other faraway places. New York was still new to us. Holidays were occurring in rapid succession. The swiftly approaching New Year was another unwanted event. With the close of 1978, I felt I was leaving Robert behind forever. New experiences had a way of separating me further from him. Then there were also the days when God seemed to hide Himself. Even the name of our little village seemed to mock us — Hopewell Junction. Yes, we had come to a junction in our lives — not a junction we anticipated or chose. We felt we had been propelled along this path and now we were groping to make something out of it. Hopewell? That was hard, but we were trying. Constantly, I reached for my Bible, and even when it seemed my Father was hidden from me, I knew that one day I would hear His voice again. Until then, His Word would remain my Friend. On one of these darkest of days, my journal records the following, written spontaneously, out of deep need:

A Cold Wintry Day
November 1978

Stripped of family, stripped of friends,
Our son has gone ahead.
Pruned and pruned, constantly cut back,
World holds no attraction,
Neither empty chatter.

Things of former days, harmless in themselves,

Are empty clutter in a life that yearns for Christ.
Needing Him, let all else go
From the list of endless activity.

What is the meaning of God's activity?
Is it because of the hastening Day?
Seeking His face, seeking His presence
In affliction, trial or prosperity;
Only let Your abiding love surround my searching spirit.

Let Your guiding Light point the chosen path;
With nothing done or said, but by Your Holy Spirit.
Sweet Comforter, surround, deepen the roots,
Bind my soul to Thee.

Let days of endless waste, empty activity,
Be days gone forever, never conjured up
To fill an empty hour.
Your grace supplies the things for which I strive.

The need for much eliminated,
My eyes have been illuminated
To see the dross.
It is not loss to lose the temporal
And gain the Spiritual.
Laying all aside, in Christ abide,
Rest in His everlasting love.

Groaning in the spirit,
Giving birth to what God desires,
Feeling pain, source unknown,
Comfort is at His feet.

My soul, be still, quietness know,
His voice to hear, His way to choose.

Strength comes to my spirit.
His peace at last.
My heart at rest.
He is the Vine,
I. . .the branch.

I am the vine, you are the branches; he who abides in
Me, and I in him, he bears much fruit; for apart from Me
you can do nothing. (John 15:5)

Thank You, Lord Jesus.

*   *   *   *   *

Divine Comfort

It was Valentine' s Day, 1979, the year I didn't want to
enter, and I woke up that morning from a dream that was so
crystal clear and explicit I will never forget it. This was also
exactly six months since the August day we stood holding
hands at Lincoln Memorial Park and was the first time I
dreamt about Bob. Six months and the ache was still heavy
in my heart. But on this day, God sent me another uplifting,
healing gift for which I will always be giving Him thanks.

Sitting around the kitchen table we were having the usual
Muthmann after-meal discussion, but Robert was with us.
He was totally enthusiastic and exuberant, looking as though
he had just returned from some South Pacific paradise.

Suddenly it came to me, "Ask what you've been
wanting to know."

So I did. "Bob, what is it like? What are you experiencing? What have you been enjoying so much?"

"Oh, Mom," came his excited reply, "It's the presence
of Jesus. Keep running the race, seeking the presence of the
Lord—that is what it is all about. It is absolutely wonderful,

I can't describe it, in fact there aren't words that could tell you."

His face and gestures were animated and lively. "I want to tell you this, and always remember it: It is worth it all. It is so worth it. No matter what you go through, if there are trials, suffering, pain, discouragement or disappointment, it is worth it. You remember the Scripture, 'He that dwells in the secret place of the Most High, shall abide under the shadow of the Almighty' (Psalm 91:1). That's where I am, and you can be there, too. That's why it's written in the Bible, all you have to do is seek the face of Jesus and we'll be there together."

He stopped a moment, then said, "I want to pray for you and Dad."

He began to pray and I wanted to give him one more hug, and as I reached for him, I woke up. Not to disappointment that he was gone, on the contrary, I was ready now for new life; enthusiasm and zest for living that life came over me in a way that I had not felt for six months. It was as though God was again holding out the gift of life to me and saying, "Here it is—life. Take it, use it, it's from Me."

And I wanted to sing:

When we've been there ten thousand years,
Bright shining as the sun
We've no less days to sing His praise
Than when we first begun.
— Yes, Robert, Together!

That same morning I went as a newcomer to a ladies' Bible Study. I knew only the hostess. There were about ten to twelve ladies and I walked in late. As I sat down someone across the room was describing her own private fear, which was: "What would I do, how would I handle it if one of my children died? I just couldn't survive! I would think

God was punishing me." She was obviously fearful and dabbed her eyes.

I thought, *Is this the reason I am here today?* The room was quiet, seemed no one knew what to say. The hostess, my friend Sharon who had sat with me many times during my grief, looked my way as if telling me to say something.

Swallowing several times, I gathered my courage and said, "I believe I am right now living through what you dread. But I want to tell you, Jesus can meet every need for each person in just the way we need it. His Love reaches beyond what we can ever imagine. Carolee, God does not punish by taking our children. He disciplines, but not that way. Let me tell you what just happened to me very early this morning. . ." and I shared my so-recent dream that was such a fresh memory. By the time I finished we were in each other's arms comforting one another. There were tears, too. Not only was God's comfort for me, but comfort for me to pass on as He showed me, even that very day.

God, undeniably, is the Workman, for "we are His workmanship, created in Christ Jesus for good works, which God prepared beforehand, that we should walk in them" (Ephesians 2:10). It certainly is not our plan, neither are we supervising our own way. He works, makes, causes, forms, and directs—we yield, and if we grieve, are sad, or angry; He does not punish. But in His gentle, loving way shows us how to walk through these dark ways. He has said it, so let's believe it!

At home I had been searching the Bible for God's further comfort for me. Just as Robert said, I found his exhortation especially in Romans 8:18, "For I consider that the sufferings of this present time are not worthy to be compared with the glory that is to be revealed to us." In 2 Corinthians 4:17, "For momentary, light affliction is producing for us an eternal weight of glory far beyond all comparison." It may sound as though the writer is making light of affliction, but, when we stop and consider all our varied trials in view of the "glorious forever" awaiting us, we can at least begin to think that anything difficult is light by comparison.

One day, with Robert's Bible in hand, I opened to James 1 and opposite the second verse he had written in the margin in large letters (just so I wouldn't miss the message!) COUNT ALL JOY. This, of course, was for him, but God knew I needed it, too. I looked at the verse, which says, "Consider it all joy. . . when you encounter various trials" (James 1:2). Only God can show us these things, and enliven His Word to us at just the time we need it, whether it is preparation or during the grieving and healing process. Whole-heartedly we can say, "Blessed be the God and Father of our Lord Jesus Christ, the Father of mercies and God of all comfort; who comforts us in all our affliction. Blessed be His glorious Name forever" (2 Corinthians 1:3-4; Psalm 72:19).

Chapter Four

The Secret Place

The Secret Place

Not a thought would I take -
Be Thou my rest assured,
That I might find that Secret Place
And give up all that's treasured.
I'll walk the stony path with You -
O Savior . . .All is measured.

Not a thought would I take -
All is planned by You,
Teach me to find the Secret Place.
There is cost, 'tis true,
I'll give You all and pay the price.
O Lord. . .You make all new.

Not a thought would I take -
Be my comfort still.
For I have found that Secret Place.
Now let Your presence fill
Every corner of my being.
O Jesus. . .Not my will.

For thus says the High exalted One, who lives forever, whose name is Holy, "I dwell in the high and holy place and also with the contrite and lowly of spirit. (Isaiah 57:15)

*   *   *   *   *

In His Shadow

In Africa the mother elephant places her young in her shadow until the baby is old enough to withstand the heat of the day. A wise parent!

A tender thought it is, and a picture of how the Father places us many times in the shadow away from where we would like to be, as we perceive life. "In the shadow of His wings will I rejoice" (Psalm 63:7-8). Sometimes it is the shadow of a cloud, something we perhaps don't see as a tender blessing and the way is darkened. But we need to cling to Him, for His right hand upholds us. Maybe it is a time of refining. If so, He can be trusted, and like Job we can say with confidence, "when He has tried me, I shall come forth as gold" (Job 23:10).

I will gladly, Father, with Your help, be gathered to the cover and shadow of Your wings for protection from the doubts that come from within, and the threats from without. Heavenly Father, be the shadow that enfolds me in Your love.

"I take, O cross, thy shadow for my abiding place;
I ask no other sunshine than the sunshine of His face;
Content to let the world go by, to know no gain nor loss,
My sinful self my only shame, my glory all the cross!"
We can sing as a prayer this beautiful hymn
by Elizabeth C. Clephane.

*   *   *   *   *

Where Do You Stay?

And Jesus turned, and beheld them following, and said to them, "What do you seek?" And they said to Him, "Rabbi, where are You staying?" He said to them, "Come and you will see." They came therefore and saw where He was staying; and they stayed with Him that day. . . . (John 1:38-39)

This can be a daily, early morning prayer:

"Where do You stay today, Lord Jesus?"

"Come and see, you can be with Me all the day. Come, follow Me today."

He is with me, I am with Him, all day, every day, nighttime, too. Prayer becomes an all-day conversation with the One who calls me Friend. It is a "stay with Me, abide with Me" way of living that makes short work of frustration, negative thoughts, attitudes, and confused emotions. He will balance our footing when we quiver and shake, even when we consciously have Him close by our side all the time. We can ask the Holy Spirit to remind us to keep the focus.

Remember when Peter asked Jesus who was walking on the water, "Lord, if it is You, command me to come to You on the water" (Matthew 14:28). I can imagine Peter all excited as he climbed out of the boat; then he was walking on water. Oh, no, he lost his focus as he caught sight of the wind or waves, and began to falter. So it happens to us when things are going well, we are following the Lord's direction, then something comes along to distract us or cause us a doubt, and we are calling for Jesus, "Save me!" But He is beside us all the time, just as He was right there with and for Peter.

I shall make the place of My feet glorious. (Isaiah 60:13)

Let us go to His dwelling place. Let us worship at His footstool. (Psalm 132:7)

Listening to the Lord's word, seated at His feet. (Luke 10:39)

*   *   *   *   *

The Oyster and Her Outrage

Perhaps you are the owner of a lovely string of pearls or pearl jewelry, and enjoy the soft, translucence of that gem from the sea. Have you thought behind the pearl or talked to the oyster? That's where we have to go today—to the oyster. She has something to tell us—an important lesson.

Think of the oyster in the depths of the ocean. One day she woke up to the annoying presence of a minute grain of sand. She conferred with herself, "I will simply ignore it, and it will go away." She waited and waited, but, no, it didn't make any difference. Then she had a new idea, "I will kick it out of my house." But as much as she tried, she just couldn't get a foothold. A few days later, after her mind had been working on the problem of this continuous irritation, she decided to move away, thinking she would be able to just leave him behind. She lurched along to a more comfortable place. It was a long journey, and she was near despair when she realized the grain of sand was still with her. "I know what I will do. I will go watch the dolphins at play and that will take my mind off this torment." It had become more than an annoyance, it was now a torment; even the dolphins didn't help her forget the obstinate presence of the intruder. Scratching her thinker, it came to her, "Ah, I will have a party and call all my friends, then the grain of sand will find out I am too busy for him. He will find someone else to irritate." Her friends came, they feasted, they played, they swam, and they danced. But, no, the irritator was still there. "What shall I do? I don't forget it. I can't ignore it, and I have no way of getting it out of my life. Will I have to live with it until the day I die?"

Now, feeling very sorry for herself; she brooded, she fretted, she got angry, and moody. Finally, it occurred to her that surely the grain of sand *was* here to stay. There was no way except to live with it. That is when she said, "I will do something that doesn't make any sense. I will keep it. I will even say, 'It's okay, you can stay with me. It doesn't sound right, but I don't know how to ask you in any other way to leave'." It came about that she began to embrace it. "I will pour out my kindness on it."

From that day on, day after day, the oyster was kind to the grain of sand. It became a habit. She wrapped it with her nacre. Like a covering, it softly embraced the tiny grain of sand. Every day a bit more, and she thought for a while that she would not have enough nacre for even one more day. At times she felt annoyed; but the next day there was more nacre for the grain of sand, and then more and more. After many days, the grain of sand lost some of its ability to irritate. The oyster began to be happy. She began to be thankful. She began to think that something wonderful was happening. And it was!

One day the deep-sea diver (the oyster had heard of such things) picked up the oyster, put it with many others and came up out of the waters. It was then that the oyster learned that in her lifetime, which had been given over to the care and acceptance of a little grain of sand, a pearl had been produced. It suddenly occurred to the oyster that her life had significance. Her life, after all, was meaningful. The worth and goal of her life was not to get rid of something irritating and clumsy, but to bring to the deep-sea diver a beautiful, translucent pearl, very costly and of unsurpassed loveliness. She thought, "Some tried to tell me that I was wasting my

life, being useless, and that I should have lived differently."
But she was learning.

The beauty of the pearl is the nacre. Layer upon layer of
nacre, a unique substance sometimes referred to as "mother
of pearl" embraces and hugs the irritant that has become part
of the life of the oyster. It is not the oyster or the irritant
where we fasten our focus or which holds the beauty. It is
the luminous layers of nacre that make the beautiful pearl.
The oyster is needed, so is the tiny grain of sand, to make
a pearl. Born in darkness, intending no good, but her surrender resulted in the very precious pearl that is part of your
lovely necklace.

Now let's bring this home to our human hardships.
Our friend Paul in 2 Corinthians 12 tells us of his personal
dilemma. He calls it a thorn in the flesh (verse 7), which
doesn't sound like something to be pleased about. In verse
10 he says, "So for the sake of Christ, I am well-pleased and
take pleasure in infirmities, insults, hardships, persecutions,
perplexities, and distresses; for when I am weak (in human
strength), then I am (truly) strong - able, powerful - in divine
strength" (AMP). Let's ask him the obvious question: How
did you get to that place of being pleased and accepting of
these kinds of intrusions? It looks impossible. When we find
ourselves in one of those extremely painful situations, we
know we will try or pray that it be eliminated or at least
make some adjustment that it be hidden out of sight, thinking
wrongly that we can forget it.

Even though our oyster friend hadn't any notion of what
nacre is or how to get it, she was capable of giving forth something that would relieve her suffering and at the same time
produce a rare and beautiful gem. Paul heard from his Father
who said to him, "My grace - My favor and loving-kindness
and mercy are enough for you (that is, sufficient against
any danger and to enable you to bear the trouble manfully);
for My strength and power are made perfect - fulfilled and

completed and show themselves most effective - in (your) weakness. Therefore," Paul says, "I will all the more gladly glory in my infirmities, that the strength and power of Christ, the Messiah, may rest - yes, may pitch a tent (over) and dwell - upon me!" (2 Corinthians 12:9-19 AMP).

It seems to me that the beauty of our life is grace, the grace of our Lord Jesus Christ. The common definition that we have heard about grace is simply unmerited favor. However in this Amplified Version we get a much fuller idea. What are all these unmerited favors? Does it include what I desperately need right now? Philippians 4:19 tells us of the fullness of the treasure house to which we are heirs. "My God shall supply all you need according to His riches in glory by Christ Jesus." Wouldn't you say that is a very full treasure house? Wealth untold in our Lord Jesus Christ, who says to us, "Whatever you ask in My name, that will I do, that the Father may be glorified in the Son. If you ask Me anything in My name, I will do it" (John 14:13-14). In John 1:16 we learn, "of His fullness we have all received, and grace upon grace."

Layer upon layer of grace, whether it is His love, power, strength, kindness or mercy, it embraces and hugs the outrage. It could be of illness, tragedy, disfigurement, or disappointment that is part of our life. It is not "I or the outrageous whatever" that holds the beauty. It has to be the luminous layers of grace that show forth in living our life, as the song says: "Let the beauty of Jesus be seen in me." Our attention is drawn to Jesus, the Pearl of great price, since He is the One who works all things according to His will and His good pleasure. By His grace, that which we first resented or found distasteful, begins to be beautiful in our eyes because we see His wisdom, His faithfulness, His power, and His leading. In this distressing circumstance we even see His glory! In the cross that He asks us to carry, our eyes are opened to see something incredibly lovely, even a blessing.

For you were called for the very purpose that you might inherit a blessing. (1 Peter 3:9)

Being willing, yielded and with acceptance, we can see victory and triumph come out of tragedy. This is the lesson from our friend the oyster, who struggled against the intruder. It is learned in the Secret Place of His Presence. With every hardship He draws us closer to Himself and our precious Savior is glorified. It was during my college days, when Dr. Rayburn addressed us daily in chapel with enlightenment from the Psalms, that I first learned the meaning of Psalm 18:11 and 104:3, "He makes the darkness His secret place, and He makes the clouds His chariot." You can add to those Micah 7:8, "Though I dwell in darkness, the Lord is a light for me."

Maybe you have read about Madam Guyon. She lived in the sixteen hundreds and carried many crosses. She learned the priceless lesson of deeper and deeper intimacy with Jesus with every cross she was to bear, and it was not a few, it was many. She was even loathe to part with one of her crosses, though her life was extremely difficult. She testifies that she was always drawn closer to Jesus with every added cross.

It is also true that the properties of the pearl include softness in contrast to other gems which are strengthened by immense heart and pressure. Pearls also have the ability to absorb light and reflect light. It seems reasonable to say that these attributes correspond to Christians when we are walking close to Jesus; yielding to His touch, receiving His wisdom, absorbing light from His Word, and reflecting His light in our lives.

When the darkness surrounds, worry sets it, and the pit is so deep, don't forget His love for you is an everlasting love. Your feelings may not support this, but looking into His Word and just saying with faith, "Lord Jesus, I trust you," He will draw you into His Secret Place to learn His ways, and receive His grace in whatever form it is needed. He will keep the strength, power, patience, kindness or courage coming, and even pitch a tent and dwell closely with you. Here is a word for all of us at all times. "I have loved you with an everlasting love; therefore I have drawn you with loving-kindness" (Jeremiah 31:3). Love, like nacre, is a covering (1Peter 4:8). So by faith, receive love and any other grace you need; these are yours, through Christ Jesus, our Lord.

"Jehovah Jireh, my Provider,
His grace is sufficient for me, for me, for me.
Jehovah Jireh, my Provider,
His grace is sufficient for me.
My God shall supply all my need,
According to His riches in glory.
He shall give His angels charge over me,
Jehovah Jireh cares for me, for me, for me.
Jehovah Jireh cares for me."

By Merla Watson

*   *   *   *   *

The Gift of Grace

Grace is God's gift to you, but to use it, you must appropriate it. You can challenge the anxiety, the tension, the short, hurtful responses through grace. God knows how much you need grace to soothe the big things and the little petty annoyances, the continuous and unending interruptions that disturb and rob life of its sweetness and peace.

Let grace, like the gentle dew in the morning garden, refresh those dried out, tired feelings that cling to you and clog your communion with your Father and with Jesus. His grace is the "change agent." It is free, reach for it, and ask for it as you sit with Jesus for a while.

For the Lord longs to be gracious to you; He rises to show you compassion. (Isaiah 30:18)

Above all, keep fervent in your love for one another, because love covers a multitude of sins. (1 Peter 4:8)

Only a few days after writing these pages, I was the observer of this very thing unfolding in the doctor's office. Shiona had been troubled about something that occurred at the day program she attends. After about a week of hearing herself rehearse this incident repeatedly, and not being able to get passed the unwelcome feelings, she decided it was time to talk to her doctor.

After a brief retelling, the doctor offered some help in the way of relaxation techniques. When she described what she had in mind, Shiona said she was hesitant, because she was afraid it could lead to something like hypnosis. So the patient doctor asked if she ever just sat still and put her thoughts in some peaceful location that she remembered well and could recapture the feelings of peace and rest.

"Oh, yes, I have often done that, Doctor," she replied. "After my brother died, many times I have thought about a place where there is a crystal sea."

"A what, Shiona?" the doctor asked.

"A crystal sea, Doctor. There are angels, and many beautiful things in that place," she said with her eyes closed, perhaps in silent prayer, about the loveliness she experienced.

Then she opened her eyes and added, "You can read all about this in Revelation. You see, I love Jesus. I know He loves me, and I know I will see my brother again."

She kept talking until she had said all that was in her heart about her Savior. It seemed that she was digging very deep in her heart, discovering again the tools with which to refresh herself from all the hurts, wounds, and disappointments she was feeling.

"Shiona, I can see that in telling me this, you already feel better," the doctor observed. "Why don't you just continue in what you are doing? I am sure you will be helped by your own spiritual way of seeing things."

Whether the doctor realized it or not, she confirmed to Shiona that she already knew the tools that were her help! *Thank You, Jesus!*

Shiona asked if she could sing a song and the doctor agreed. She stood up and sang a couple of spontaneous songs, finishing with Barry McGuire's, "Bullfrogs and the butterflies, they've both been born again." Then she reached out to shake hands with her doctor saying, "Thank you, Doctor, for letting me talk to you, today. I feel better."

She went into the doctor's office in agony, she left in ecstasy! As we walked to the elevator she told me, "I know where my help is; Jesus is my Helper!"

"Yes, Shiona," I confirmed to her, "I believe you found out that no matter what, you're standing on the solid Foundation!"

Making pearls! Every day we probably have more opportunities than we take advantage of in the making of pearls. Let's be diligent and ask for His help in each time of need. If we do so, we will soon be handing our Deep Sea Diver a whole handful of pearls!

Love Grows
Love Covers
because
God is Love
God so Loved
(1 Thessalonians 3:12; 1 Peter 4:8; I John. 4:7, 3:16)

* * * * *

Alone with Jesus

The still small voice -
In the valley
In the desert.

Heard in the solitary -
In the quiet
In the stillness.

Away from the crowd -
Of nagging thoughts
Of endless questions.

I hear His voice -
Come unto Me
I will come to you

In the stillness -
I have called you by your name
You are Mine.

In His fellowship -
Take My yoke
Find my rest.

(Matthew 11:28; John 14:28; Isaiah 45:4;
John 17:10-11; Isaiah 43:1; Matthew 11:28-29)

* * * * *

A Lesson from the Secret Place

Jesus said, "Blessed are your eyes, because they see; and your ears, because they hear" (Matthew 13:16). Having eyes that see and ears that hear are the very reason to have a secret place where, in quiet, we can listen to our Savior, then see and understand what He has in mind for us each day. We can be ever so thankful because even the darkness is not dark to Him, and the night (that sometimes surrounds us) is as bright as the day. Darkness and light are as one to Him. For this I am thankful, because I know He is here and knows all (Psalm 139:12), and is willing to give understanding and insight. The prophet Isaiah tells of those who hear, but don't understand and have closed their eyes to God. How thankful we should be, being so blessed.

O Lord, help me see and help me listen in this time with You in the secret place.

"The Lord has need of them," Jesus said to the disciples when He sent them for a donkey and her foal (Matthew 21:3). He needed the donkey to carry Him to Jerusalem. A very precious thought that the Lord of the universe, the Creator of all things even the donkey, had this need. The disciples obeyed, the donkey with her foal obeyed.

Obedience for the long term, for the long haul, has value from God's point of view that we absolutely do not understand. Beyond what our burden or duty is there is a certain accomplishment that takes place. For one thing it brings a strengthening of our faith and also purifies our motives as it restores our focus.

My thoughts are not your thoughts, neither are My ways your ways, says the Lord. (Isaiah 55:8-9)

The Lord also says, "To obey is better than sacrifice" (1 Samuel 15:22). Obedience is a constant call as opposed to giving up something which makes it easy to say, "Now, let's get on with life." Rather, obedience teaches us to stay the course. It is saying, "I delight to do Thy will, O Lord" (Psalm 40:8). If we saw the long road ahead we might just say, "No, not for me." But thankfully, He doesn't show us the whole road. I am very thankful that God held the curtain closed on future events in our lives, and just like the manna, He always gave us just enough for each day, and only what was best for us.

Remember when the people wandered in the desert and gathered daily manna? Some folks got the idea to gather extra, as though working ahead of God meant they could have more time the next day for their own ideas. Well, God cured that. On the next day the manna saved was foul and had to be disposed of. If we had too much for one day, God knows we would like to give up and let the life He chose for us wither in our overanxious arms. He is the Father who knows what's best for His children. Let's learn that lesson soon, and go often to the secret place to spend time waiting with Him to bless our eyes and ears in learning to be obedient children. Obedience brings conflict. We cannot overlook this because the ways of God are not our ways, and His ways are not the ways of the world. So we endure contradiction and it is the more painful when the work He has given us conflicts with the organized church system or with family members. Let's face it, and I did not want to face this, churches in some cases have not learned compassion very well. Jesus said, "I desire compassion, not sacrifice" (Matthew 9:13). It is easier to sit down and write a check than to spend time learning compassion, which doesn't always come easily.

Granted, for some people it is natural to be a care-giver. I don't happen to subscribe to that group of people. Jesus had many things to teach me and I did not like all the lessons for quite some time. I had to go again to Philippians 2:13, "For it is God who is at work in you, both to will and to do of

His good pleasure." He had to keep pointing me in the right direction. Repetition is not always fun, but it is one of the best teachers!

Now I think I have to tell you something about myself. First of all, I never wanted to be a nurse or be educated in the medical field. When I was about to graduate from high school my aunt kept telling me how noble the nursing profession was but it never resonated with me. I think I truly disappointed her. Give me a book, a pencil and paper, some fabric to work with or any other raw material, and I can make myself happy all day long. The music lessons I managed to tolerate all my education years became thoroughly enjoyable. I discovered, too, my harp practice was many times soothing to Shiona on difficult days. Now I see the Lord has been teaching me for many years and He has led me far beyond natural gifts. I have learned to navigate through sixteen prescriptions, keep it all straight, including two kinds of insulin, as well as administering everything.

At times, though still not every time, I may be able to say, "Yes, Lord, with Your help I believe I can please You in this interruption." This has been a life long journey for me, but what I have learned about my Savior and my Father far exceeds any expectations. Repeatedly, you will catch me referring to Philippians 2:13. That word has been a stabilizer since my teen years. This is not to say that I have arrived; to the contrary.

Ask Jay and he will tell you, "Janet still has her 'Irish' moments."

As a result, there are many confessions to my Father. The house I have given to Jesus, but I still am not quite used to disarray, however, it does get orderly! There are seasons of despair and disappointment, but let's encourage one another; Jay and Shiona know how to do that well. So we join in a song of praise to our Father and sing, "Thou art my God and I will praise Thee, Thou art my God I will exalt Thee. Oh give thanks unto the Lord, for He is good and His mercy endureth forever!" (Psalm 118:28-29).

Jesus said, "Learn compassion." Apparently that means He can teach us, if we would want to be so taught, and that He is not disappointed if it does not come naturally. Certainly there are many things that do not come easy. We are His body, and we are all broken; we live in a broken world. This was talked about in an earlier chapter, but we need to explore this subject in terms of special needs. Is it really necessary to say that; probably, because we all get used to our limitations. However, there are limitations that some live with that are not simple. For example, wheels for some children are not the fun wheels such as tricycles or scooters. Crutches are not Pogo sticks. Reading can mean using fingers instead of eyes. Some limitations cannot be seen, only observed because of mental limitations. These are things that cannot be glossed over, hidden, or denied. What then do we do, as His body or individually, as we work together for the good and His best for all?

Recently, an occasion brought this clearly to my mind. For instance, picture yourself in your kitchen or workshop at your house. A friend you have just met comes over for the afternoon, and wants to pitch-in and help. You chat as you work, and suddenly you notice that she/he did something that is against the rules of your orderliness. How do you handle this? You can say, "Oh, no, don't do that. We never do that here! I'll show you a better way!" Without meaning to, you may have stalled or damaged a new friendship before it ever got started because you didn't realize that your new friend is sensitive.

Within the body, we can stand back a bit and in a kind way, let whatever bothers us happen a few times until we get a handle on how he/she is likely to respond. We have all done this perhaps just because we are eager, but the person we are talking about probably needed a more careful approach so we must slow down. Just as on the highway, the caution signs slow us down because men are working on the road. It cripples our progress, but if we don't follow the instructions we shouldn't be surprised to find ourselves in a big mess.

Maybe the person has a strong need to feel included, wanted, and encouraged before he/she can begin to absorb your methods of operation. It takes time to catch up. What is the important factor here? Isn't it to be included?

Consider this conversation that was overheard at church one Sunday after the service. Someone with special needs said to the pastor, "I would like to become a member." Yes, it was a blunt remark, without any verbal preamble. Could be that it was also a repeat request, but it was dismissed with, "Well, what are you trying to do, pull one on me again?" Sounds like a thoughtless brush-off. What would the family do? Try another church, stay home, or remain on the fringe, outside the benefits of membership? Why not sit down, have a chat, learn the limitations that excluded this one from fellowship or made friendliness awkward. Why not offer your friendship?

Sometimes we honor our own title or position, when Jesus tells us we need to have His attitude in John 12:13-17, "If I then, the Lord and the Teacher, washed your feet, you also ought to wash one another's feet. For I gave you an example. . . A slave is not greater than his master. . . . If you know these things, you are blessed if you do them." Jesus even washed the feet of His betrayer! Blessed even in washing the enemy's feet? But we're talking about tender lambs with disabilities. Let's learn and receive the blessing that comes with obedience.

Time—it takes time to get passed the limitations that interrupt a person's life. We know that people with special needs are not unworthy, but we might make them feel unworthy. You know that all-too-common "hurry-up" feeling? Among the most basic needs are patience, mercy,

acknowledgement, forbearance, time, love, and apprecia-
tion. In the unworthiness of us all, God first loved us. We
love, care, and help because He first loved us. We could be
thinking the interference would mess up our own plans.

Interruptions—we don't like them. But have you traced
through the Gospels and found that Jesus' walk among us
was made up of interruptions? Have you noticed that Jesus
said He did only what His Father told Him to do? No personal agenda! Learning Jesus' ways with people is a great
way to learn the response required for people with special
needs. Think of Jesus: He willingly took time to bless the
little children. He was also aware of the impatience of His
disciples and taught by example. Can we look passed immo-
rality, alcoholism, drugs, prison records, and yet not have a
few minutes for a person with special needs? Can we go to
Africa, India, China, the jungle, and the ghetto yet ignore a
mission at home, in the neighborhood, at church, or in the
pew beside us?

The Apostle Paul compares our bodies to Christ's Body:

*Some of the parts that seem weakest and least important
are really the most necessary. Yes, we are especially
glad to have some parts that seem rather odd! And we
carefully protect from the eyes of others those parts that
should not be seen, while of course the parts that may be
seen do not require this special care. So God has put the
body together in such a way that extra honor and care
are given to those parts that might otherwise seem less
important. This makes for happiness among the parts, so
that the parts have the same care for each other that they
do for themselves. If one part suffers, all parts suffer with
it, and if one part is honored, all the parts are glad. . . .
All of you together are the one body of Christ and each
one of you is a separate and necessary part of it.* (1
Corinthians 12:22-27)

Please, stop and read that last sentence again. All of us together are the one body of Christ and each one of us is a separate and necessary part of it! This passage is a good place to study for those interested in this discussion. The idea of oneness, honor, hiddenness, prominence, suffering, protection, and care are all worthy of note. The body is a unit, so we want that inclusiveness for all.

Of course, we are not suggesting that everyone is going to be a care-giver or have a hands-on-ministry. God chooses and God guides. The expectation must be toward Him (Psalm 62:5). Some will be back-up and support while others are in the front lines. This is true in all ministry in Christ's Body.

Care-givers have had a comprehensive education. Talk to one someday. You can learn, too. They can give you ideas and insight. You will also be amazed at the blessing that comes to you in this care-giving ministry. Does all this frighten you away? Remember how Paul exhorts us to never give up.

Though our bodies are dying, our inner strength in the Lord is growing every day. These troubles and sufferings of ours (including people with special needs) *are, after all, quite small and won't last very long. Yes, this short time of distress will result in God's richest blessing upon us forever and ever!* (2 Corinthians 4:16-17 TLB).

You can even read this to your new friend who has special needs, and both be encouraged. You can explain that you, too, have needs, not like your friend, but you may feel weak, discouraged, or troubled in some way. These verses are for all kinds of suffering that God's people go through. We all have to ask Jesus for strength, patience, endurance, and many other things. He is wise and will graciously equip us whether we need Him because we have special needs or we are helpers to those with special needs. He is our all-knowing, all-wise Father.

Here's an idea list for starters in this adventure:

- Read to or with your friend, an appropriate book or magazine in his/her interest area.
- Help your friend write a note or letter. Even make the card or stationery together, recycling used cards.
- Learn some songs together - he/she could surprise you by being musically gifted. Perhaps he/she could teach you a new song. It might be that you will bring a new song or step or any small thing of newness to his/her life. To that person it will be marvelous indeed.
- Go for a ride, grab a drink or treat at a favorite place. Sometimes folks like to get away from the family and tiresome, familiar surroundings for a while.
- Play a game; make up a new game.
- Maybe your new friend would like to sit with you at church for a change.
- Think, as you observe your friend's needs, of something you could do or supply that would ease his/her uneasiness. Once I observed a father take a straw out of his pocket as Communion was being served so that his son with special needs could take the grape juice more easily. A very kind gesture.
- Don't be put-off by inappropriate comments or questions. He/she is not trying to annoy you; it is a learning situation for them, too.
- Smiles and giggles make for happy, easy-going times. "A merry heart does good like a medicine" (Proverbs 17:22 KJV).
- For yourself, treat this as an excellent learning time as you put in practice the scripture that says, "My soul, wait thou only upon God; for my expectation is from Him" (Psalm 62:5).

It would only take two or three church members, the Elders and Pastor to have some time together, looking at possibilities within the body to launch a meaningful program for a few folks with special needs. Only God knows the far-reaching effects of such a ministry. Someone in the church might already know of a church that has a well-functioning group, and without a doubt they would help you get started. Don't let the multiple blessings be withheld from those in need or from yourselves and your church body.

I have learned of one pastor who invites people with special needs to "come up front and sing" or to "give a testimony." He helps them get started with something like, "Hey, how was your week? Have any blessings to share?" You will be surprised to see the results of purposeful inclusion as tensions relax. It's not difficult to love hungry people. Watch the excitement as the feeling of, "I belong" grows and joy overflows from the heart. God will surely bless you in this opportunity to extend Jesus' command, "Feed My lambs."

*   *   *   *   *

Wanting to pass on the songs that Jesus had been giving her, Shiona was longing to have an audience just to share her joy. While we were taking a walk in the mall, I heard this over and over. Knowing we couldn't snap our fingers to produce an audience, we just kept on walking. However, coming around the corner toward a seating area, we saw a group of people. We looked and there right in front of us was a group of about thirty persons with special needs. Did she need an invitation or an introduction? No! She didn't even think about that.

Shiona just walked boldly to the front of the group and asked, "Would you like me to sing for you?"

"Yes, yes," came the instant response, their excitement was not hidden!

Her purse and a couple of packages went to the floor as she stepped forward to begin this unexpected concert! As she finished the second or third song, she stopped a moment and asked if they wanted more. One young man in a wheelchair directly in front of her was making motions. She thought he wanted her to stop.

One of the care-givers answered her questioning look, "Oh, no, he just wants you to know how much he likes it and that you must sing more!"

Happily and joyfully she sang on. After several more songs we parted, but not without handshakes, high-fives, and blessings all around. Our happy young lady knew God heard her prayer, and responded with a total surprise that day. That group and that place was her answer!

So it is true, many times this "momentary, light affliction" brings with it a blessing that lasts forever and forever. We are invited to this blessing when we look around, and in happy obedience, carry Jesus to the ones He sends us to!

Relate this concept now to the donkey story. What if the disciples had not been obedient to the Lord's request? What if Shiona had backed away from her Creator? We might think we would have said, "I would gladly have been there for Jesus!" But He gives us the very opportunity many times in the pew beside us or in the neighborhood, the mall or the hospital. Jesus is a good and patient teacher. Let's not back away from learning to carry Him to the persons of special needs or spiritual needs. My daughter is the one whom the Lord has used to teach me. Admittedly, I used to pull back wondering as I tried to understand her ease with people. Now I believe this is God's gift to her and her joy is visible.

Consider this story that happened on a particular Sunday when I was there to watch one of the first occasions of Shiona's unique way of ministering to a friend. It was a large Sunday School class of persons with special needs. About forty or more students were sitting in a very wide circle.

After some group singing, Shiona got up from her seat and walked across the wide circle to stand in front of Robbie. Everyone was watching as this was all very spontaneous.

A drooling problem meant that Robbie always wore a colorful bandana around his neck. On this day he seemed a little excited and Shiona caught on. She noticed that he was wearing a brand new bandana. To make the occasion special for Robbie and his new bandana, she had a song for him. As she sang, we all saw the expression of joy on his face. The joy was contagious and all joined in. Robbie has difficulty expressing himself, but that day, beyond any doubt, he was celebrating. The teacher told me that it was the first time she had ever seen Robbie smile. We will never forget Robbie's "New Bandana Day" as we often speak of that special occasion. Of course, it was merely a momentary incident and in a way a reminder of Jesus' observation when the widow offered the two small coins that probably no one else noticed. Jesus sees the smallest impulse, and if we don't "see" as Jesus "sees" we miss the blessing of, "Little is much when God is in it." A good word to remember when the only thing we can do, seems so trivial. Yet a caring, trivial gesture can make a very joyful moment. Quickly the joy on Robbie's face raced around the room, and we were all enjoying the joy of being enjoyed by Jesus! Remember, it is all for His good pleasure! Our Father wants something from us. He wants to see us transformed into the image of His Son. That is exactly where He is taking us, and He will accomplish it as we yield to His directions. Joy is a big part of it!

To obey God is to know God. Obedience brings us closer to the Father. Daniel 11:32 makes this real, "They that do know their God shall be strong and do exploits." I had to read this a few times and concentrate to really hear it with my ears open. Sharply aware of the circumstances surrounding us, I wanted this to be significant in our endeavors. Then I captured the initial step; to obey God is to know God! When we know God we are doing (obeying) His will. He is making us aware of what He wants done. Moreover, we are finished with working *for* God and begin working *with* God. We have then crossed the line and put selfishness behind us. If there are days we slip up, He is faithful and just to forgive and cleanse us.

Jesus is saying, "I need you to carry out My will in this very situation of your circumstances."

"Help me, Lord, to respond to You in an attitude of heart that is pleasing to You and through which Your desires and plans are accomplished. I would be humble, unselfish and obedient to You, Lord of all. You search and know me. You know when I sit down in despair, and when I rise up strong in spirit and resolve because You understand my thoughts from afar. You scrutinize my path and You are intimately acquainted with all my ways. How precious also are Your thoughts to me, my God, my Savior. Keep calling me, drawing me to Your ways, and enlighten my understanding. Thank You, Father."

* * * * *

Learn of Me

"The very life of the wounded cries for help"
Job 24:12 AMP.

Dear Lord, teach me . . .
To die to the words that beckon utterance
from a mother's lips,
words that would only cripple and crush a fragile soul.

Dear Lord, help me . . .
To stop the spewing forth though driven from ear-
nesst passion

for truth and aorrectness, for You have said,
"Let be, and know that I am God." (Psalm 46:10 AMP)

I will wait, and I will see
how much more loving and kind is Your grace
when poured forth like oil
on a troubled mind.

"There is therefore now no condemnation.
For the law was given through Moses:
(to keep lepers away, even the woman with a flow of blood):
But grace and truth came by Jesus Christ." (Romans 8:1,
John 1:17KJV)

How precious is His blood.
See how He calls us through grace, His grace.
Can I not follow Him more closely
and learn His gentle touch?

Dwelling Places

A place of rest — a place of peace
A place of prayer — and a place of praise
A place of thanksgiving — and joy
A place of feasting and fellowship.

A place of trust — and service
A place of cleansing — a place of healing
A place of protection and of strength
A place of acceptance — a place of love
A place of freedom — and refreshing.

A place of repentance and forgiveness
A place of commission and blessing
A place of sacrifice — a place of abundance

A place of guidance and of hope.

A place to hide — a place to wait
A place of fruitfulness — a place of glory.

In Him we live, we move, we have our being. (Acts 17:28)

How lovely are Thy dwelling places, O Lord. (Psalm 84:1)

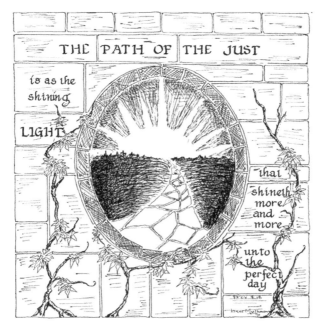

THE PATH OF THE JUST is as the shining LIGHT that shineth more and more unto the perfect day

Prov. 4:18

Chapter Five

His Way Is Perfect

Rough Road Ahead

We didn't know, but God knew that we were about to embark on a more rugged path. There was no sign that said, "Road to Troubled Waters" or "Steep Grade Ahead," nor any other warning. So we went on as we usually did, praying and waiting for significant direction. Robert had now been in his new Home for about three years. Following our heart's yearnings we moved from New York back to Portland, Oregon. It would be good to be near old friends, including Robert's friends who had spent so much time in our home. We missed the fellowship we had grown to love in Portland and followed that direction. After five months of renewing our fellowship with those we loved, God made it plain that Portland was not the place for us. Contact with Jay's former company seemed to indicate a new opportunity, and life in Kansas City, Missouri was something we could welcome.

The move to the mid-west was not totally foreign to us, since Jay and I met while attending Covenant College, at that time located in St. Louis. Still, making a home in Kansas City was another stretch for all of us. Even in the three years since Robert died, Shiona had not found relief from the loneliness for her brother. She had graduated from High School in New York, enjoyed our short time in Portland, and since our move to Kansas City she'd found work at Sears. However, underlying anxiety was stressing her out. Robert's death, the move, her first job were all reasons for a counselor. She thought some medication might help and told him so. Nevertheless, he was not in agreement. It wasn't long after that when she called me from work needing an urgent ride home. She was stressed beyond the ability to help herself, even though her counselor had been so sure she could. Jay was not traveling nearly as often as formerly, but for this emergency he was on a business trip.

I prayed, "God, help us."

I picked her up at Sears and got to her counselor's office before closing time. He spent four hours trying to make her understand she could help herself. At nine o'clock he came out of his office to give me the name and phone number of a psychiatrist and hospital. We endured an agonizing night decidedly different from the sleepless night when Robert died. It was very hard to hide my anxieties while striving to keep her troubled thoughts in check and her fears at bay. I disconnected all the phones, tried to explain that her driver's license and high school diploma were valid, and she didn't need to turn herself in to the police. She was unsure about everything. I sat up with her all night as neither of us closed our eyes.

By the time the horrific night ended, I knew she had lost it. We were not connecting. At 7 a.m. we got in the car. It was a thirty-five mile drive to the hospital in a town I had never been to before. We barely got started when she spotted a police car and opened the car door to get out. In her altered state of mind, she thought she had to turn herself in. Catching the door before she could jump or fall out, I held the door locked with my right hand, while steering with my left hand, for the forty-five minute drive. I was alarmed, having never seen someone in such a state ever. Needless to say, I prayed the whole way.

When I asked the doctor what the problem was, all she said was, "She is psychotic!" She looked at me as if to say, "Isn't that obvious?"

Probably I knew but did not want to admit the obvious. Shiona was placed in isolation. I was stupefied, and my inner pain was indescribable. WHY? WHY? WHY? In my helplessness I had to leave her there. Never had I been so torn apart. Isolation meant I could only mouth the words of my heart, "Goodbye, my sweet girl, I love you," at the one tiny window where only part of her face and frightened eyes were visible. It was a silent drive home with the words, "I couldn't even give her a hug," repeating in my head.

At 7:00 a.m. the next morning the hospital called, "Come right away, Shiona won't eat or drink, she is dehydrating. We need your help and permission to admit her to the Community Hospital!"

Amazed that they needed my help, I hurried through the heavy morning traffic. After getting her by ambulance to the medical hospital, I spent the rest of the day with her. Kind friends whom we had met a short time before, drove down to get my car keys then located and brought my car from the psychiatric hospital to the medical hospital so I could drive back home. *Father, bless them for that kindness!*

A few days later she needed to be readmitted to the psychiatric hospital, but she was not wanted. It took at least a day and a half to convince them that her father held an important position with an international company of excellent reputation, and they would be assured of their money. Through it all with prayer and waiting, God made the way. I will never forget the peace that came over me. It truly was "the peace that passes all understanding," (Philippians 4:7). I was experiencing one of the "treasures" that come in the bundle of life when the road is rough and hidden.

Many and varied were the hospital experiences, both for Shiona and for us. We were in training, Jay and I. We didn't know what or how many years of learning were ahead for us. Learning almost everything over again was the agenda for Shiona. Life has never come fully back for her. But that is saying we know better than God, which we don't! Some things were slowly coming back, and many skills took longer than others. She was often frustrated and lonely. There was much to learn about doctors, hospitals, medicine, routines, and scheduling. We learned about steady, continuous prayer; praying always. Shiona was learning, too.

One of the staff at the psychiatric hospital said to me one day, "You know, I sit with Shiona every evening before she goes to bed and she always prays for the staff, for the cooks, the nurses, and the other patients. She really blesses me with her caring thoughts for others."

The time for her release finally came. Her discharge after four and a half months seemed deserving of a proper parting, so the hospital threw a party. Everyone was invited; doctors, staff, and patients. Shiona sang for them, her music therapist accompanied her with guitar. Her voice at this time, and for quite a few months, was tiny and high pitched and expressed no emotion. Here are the words she sang, the song is from Sr. Miriam T. Winter:

I saw raindrops on my window,
Joy is like the rain.
Laughter runs across my pain,
Slips away and comes again,
Joy is like the rain.

I saw clouds upon a mountain,
Joy is like a cloud.
Sometimes silver, sometimes gray,

Always sun not far away.
Joy is like a cloud.

I saw Christ in wind and thunder,
Joy is tried by storm.
Christ asleep within my boat,
Whipped by wind, yet still afloat.
Joy is tried by storm.

I saw raindrops on the river,
Joy is like the rain,
Bit by bit the river grows,
'Till all at once it overflows.
Joy is like the rain.

The third stanza especially brought tears to my eyes. Some things to wonder about came to my mind. Would the joy come back? How long would it take? There would be many things that we would want to see back; her smile, bright eyes, voice, spontaneity, joyful countenance, but when? Her voice was quiet, weak, and thin. Her face was without emotion. As she sang this song, the emotion was in the faces in front of her. There were few dry eyes.

One of the staff came to me afterward to tell me something I will never forget, "This hospital will never be the same since Shiona came here!" *Thank You, Father.*

One of the doctors asked her, "What brought you through, Shiona?"

Her one word answer, "Love."

This was something else I would never forget. Yet her expression was still blank.

The next ten years brought three more hospitalizations. Each time the doctors either didn't catch the signs or they became complacent and suggested stopping the medicine. We were told a variety of diagnoses through the years. But the one that has made the most sense is the connection that one doctor made with the head injury of years ago when Shiona was only seven. That, with the epilepsy that followed shortly after, makes the most sense while other mental conditions are secondary to the brain trauma. We no longer seek a precise diagnosis. Each doctor has had his/her specific interpretation. Opinions don't indicate fact. What we observe must be dealt with regardless of the label. Since labels many times carry stigmas along with them, who needs another knock on the head?

When you first listen to the doctors you rethink everything, trying to integrate new opinions and observations with what you see and deal with 24/7. Then you go to the Lord, lay it all out before Him, ask for His guidance, His wisdom, His strength, and His peace. Next you start learning a little about trust. Doctors usually don't have any advice about trust unless you have been blessed to have a Christian doctor or they offer their credentials as trustworthy.

Now I find I am facing a real dilemma. My head says other people have been through this. Have they written about their experience? I didn't find anything helpful. So thinking about this "Rough Road" we are on, I go back in time and imagine myself in the Black Forest walking with Jay. I did not need a bigger knapsack of trust then because I trusted the Lord. I trusted Jay. Life was a wonderful adventure. At another time, it was a secure feeling hiking on an Oregon trail leading to the Pacific Ocean. Life was comfortable. But now I am imagining myself when the road is rugged and all uphill. Then comes a hairpin turn carved out of the shear side of the mountain and the road narrows to one car only. I can't see around the tight bend and Jay honks to let an unseen driver know we are coming.

That's when I say, "Stop the car! Let me out! I'd rather walk."

Then Jay abruptly says, "Don't you trust the driver?"

When you get to that place in your dilemma, it's good to have a Driver you can trust!

Then a memory comes into sharp view: Riding in the car one day with his dad, Robert had this insight at age four and a half, "Daddy, I figured out what being a Christian is like. It's like riding in a car, you don't drive, but you get there because Jesus in the Driver!"

Thank you, Robert. "Out of the mouths of babes You have established strength" (Psalm 8:2). Yes, Jesus is the Driver! He's the Driver I can trust to navigate this rough road. He shows me how to walk with Him, daily, hourly, moment by moment. He knows that right now in this critical moment I don't even know how to crawl.

Gently He talks to me, "Trust Me, you are precious to Me. Lean on Me. I know the plans I have for you, and for Shiona. Step by step I will lead you, My rod and My staff will comfort you. You won't know everything at once. But I have walked the rugged path for you. For you, I overcame!"

And I give thanks to Him, again and again!

*   *   *   *   *

Trust Me

I want to know the Way, O Lord.
Will it be rough or plain?
I cannot tell you that, My child,
But trust Me, I overcame.

I want to know the Why, O Lord,
Why did it happen so?
I cannot tell you that, dear one,
Trust Me, I'm here, I know!

95

I want to know how Long, O Lord,
How long must I endure?
I cannot tell you that, My child,
Just trust Me, My love is pure.

I want to know the End, O Lord,
What will the outcome be?
Treasures of darkness, hidden wealth,
And joy eternally!
Trust Me, My child, I overcame,
Trust Me, I overcame!

Call upon Him while He is near. . . . He will have com-
passion. . . . For My thoughts are not your thoughts,
neither are your ways My ways, declares the Lord. For
as the heavens are higher than the earth, so are My
ways higher than your ways and my thoughts than your
thoughts. (Isaiah 55:6-9)

* * * * *

The Path of the Just

Is this really the way He has chosen for me?
I question in my doubt.
He answers with His question:
"Is it not lawful for Me to do as I will with what is My
own?" (Matthew 20:15).
Then the caution, "Blessed is the one who is not offended
in Me" (Luke 7:23).

O Lord, let my weak response become stronger
and stronger
As I learn in the daily, hourly lessons to trust You
more and more.

My life seems like a patchwork,
And I feel scattered here and there,
From mountain tops, through valleys,
So often threatened by despair.

I've found the Word, it shows me
(There are road-marks on the way)
That He gathers all together
To make plain at break of Day.

In the Word I met them,
Yet they lived so long ago;
And as each one shared his story,
I could see their faces all aglow.

Years of walking through the desert
Moses found it Holy Ground,
And just beside the burning bush
There met the great I AM.

Jonah, fervently praying to God
While deep inside the fish,
Learns of God's mercy for Nineveh town
And His scorn for Jonah's wish.

Job rose from the ashes heaped
When restoration became his joy.
And youthful Isaac on the altar
In the God of Promise found his joy.

Looking back on years of prison;
Despised, forgotten, rejected, alone;
Joseph learned this priceless lesson -
Jehovah turns evil for the good of His own.

David in the valley, David in distress,
David now in sorrow, David under duress.
The secret place, the quiet place,
The place of the Strong Defender;
This was his place of calm endurance,
The place of his peaceful surrender.

Old Abraham climbed the mountain
To meet Jehovah His Provider.
To the block went John the Baptist
Now face to face with the Lamb of God.

John Apostle went to exile
Hand in hand with the God of love.
To the grave went brother Lazarus,
And met the Living God.

To each and every one
The promise is the same:
He gathers all together
To make plain at break of Day.

Is not the end greater than the beginning? Is not the end really the eternal, that *eternal weight of glory* which is far beyond all comparison to the prisons of limitation? Through the exiles of loneliness and abandonment, the valleys of despair, and the graves of bereavement, is the end greater than the beginning? Only now at this moment it is that place of *momentary light affliction* He has in His wisdom chosen for us (2 Corinthians 4:17). Saints, apostles, prophets, martyrs each had to find that safe place in our blessed Lord Jesus for the calm endurance needed for this age-long minute. The following are scriptures that have comforted me as again and again I went to His Word for strength, wisdom, and insight.

All the paths of the Lord are loving-kindness and truth.
(Psalm 25:10)

For I consider that the sufferings of this present time are not worthy to be compared with the glory that is to be revealed to us. (Romans 8:18)

Therefore we do not lose heart, but though our outer man is decaying, yet our inner man is being renewed day by day. For momentary, light affliction is producing for us an eternal weight of glory far beyond all comparison while we look not at the things which are seen, but at the things which are not seen; for the things which are seen are temporal, but the things which are not seen are eternal. (2 Corinthians 4:16-18)

Behold, I go forward but He is not there, and backward, but I cannot perceive Him; when He acts on the left, I cannot behold Him; He turns on the right, I cannot see Him. But He knows the way I take; when He has tried me, I shall come forth as gold. (Job 23:8-10)

*   *   *   *   *

Offended or Yielded?

Could it be that John the Baptist's imprisonment caused him to wonder about important questions? Loneliness, abandonment, and isolation are severe tests of one's faith. John the Baptist could not be a part of Jesus' company of disciples and followers. His work was precise: *Preparer of the Way* (John 1:23). He himself said, "He must increase, but I must decrease" (John 3:30). It was not long until John's fidelity to the truth, "Behold the Lamb of God which takes away the sin of the world" (John 1:29), cost him his life. There is no doubt about his complete and total trust in the Coming One.

Soon one event led to another until Herod was trapped and John's head was off. But having sent some disciples to Jesus before the final event, John was told the benediction of his life in Jesus' own words: "Blessed is he who is not offended in Me" (Luke 7:23). Jesus knew and confirmed that John was faithful to the end.

It is quite possible to be led in a path that appears in contradiction to the established, traditional church life. It is possible to feel abandoned, rejected, alone, isolated, and to wonder if life could not serve Jesus' purpose better in another path than the one my feet are on. (As if we could know better than our Heavenly Father!) Jesus did not rescue John the Baptist from the executioner. He did not rescue Stephen from the stones of unbelievers. Through centuries we learn of multitudes whom Jesus did not heal, deliver or preserve for this life, even though the three Hebrews were saved from fiery death and Daniel from the lions' jaws. The important thing in all of this is: "Blessed is he who is not offended in Me!"

Lord Jesus, let me respond with joy and thankfulness, because You are my Helper, I shall not be afraid.

Therefore, since we receive a kingdom which cannot be shaken, let us show gratitude, by which we may offer to God an acceptable service with reverence and awe. (Hebrews 12:28)

*   *   *   *   *

Our Father's Delays

Our Father's delays are deliberate;
He works not by our clock.
So why do we run when He says, "Walk"?

Our Father's delays are deliberate;
Have we ever marked Him, "Too late?"
So why be anxious when He says, "Wait"?

Our Father's delays are deliberate;
Being His child and never a client,
He the Source, so much more than sufficient.

Our Father's delays are deliberate;
We count delays as "too long."
But why not sing: He'll give the song!

Our Father's delays are deliberate;
Eternity being His habitat.
"Why restless?" says He. "Come, chat!"

Our Father's delays are deliberate;
A bruised reed He will not break,
"Will you not care awhile for My Sake?"

Our Father's delays are deliberate;
In His eternal leisure He looks -
Perhaps He'll find this nose in His Book!

Our Father's delays are deliberate;
He does what He deems best
And comforts, "Come unto Me and rest."

Our Father's delays are deliberate;
Is there not a reason, a worthy cause,
That patience is wrought by the lingering pause?

Our Father's delays are deliberate.
Yet, O, for a thousand tongues to sing:
"Come, Lord Jesus, come swiftly. Come!
With Your wisdom, Your presence, Your call!"

With the Lord one day is as a thousand years, and a thousand years as one day. The Lord is not slow about His promise. (2 Peter 3:8)

This I recall to my mind, therefore I have hope. The Lord's loving-kindnesses indeed never cease, for His compassions never fail. They are new every morning; great is Thy faithfulness. "The Lord is my portion," says my soul, "Therefore I have hope in Him." The Lord is good to those who wait for Him, to the person who seeks Him. It is good that he waits silently for the salvation of the Lord. (Lamentations 3:21-26)

* * * * *

Why Did You Doubt?

In their desert experience, the people asked, "Is the Lord among us or not?" (Exodus 17:7)

Certainly He was among them. They had no cause to doubt Him. We also know that when we doubt, we have lost focus. Sometimes our feeble faith lacks strength. But the problem is never on God's side. He is always faithful and worthy of trust. Could it be that in losing focus we become unwilling to believe that God is in every circumstance, every situation; even if it seems overwhelming or without solution? Then He gently reminds us to look at Him, He is there, He is here!

Even in the days of Jesus and His disciples, they doubted, they were troubled and cried out in fear. They were in the boat that Jesus told them to get into and go to the other side. But it wasn't long until they were fighting the contrariness of the elements and felt terribly afraid. As Jesus came to them He said, "Be of good cheer; it is I, be not afraid!" (Matthew 14:22-33).

In our home a charcoal sketch hangs on the wall. Sometimes it is in one room then in another, but always there as a reminder. Robert sketched it a short time before he died. It has become a distinct blessing in our home, a reminder again and again that Jesus is indeed in every situation, even the most painful ones. This sketch pictures Jesus holding Peter after his failed attempt to walk on water. Jesus is saying, "Oh you of little faith, why did you doubt?" Things were going well as he stepped out of the boat, then he looked away towards the chaos of wind and waves. Looking away from Jesus comes out of our human frailty. It is the need we have to assess the encroaching circumstances. Jesus said, "Oh you of little faith, why did you doubt?" The obvious lesson is look to Jesus for safety, comfort, peace, and strength. In Peter's mind was often repeated what Jesus said earlier, "Be of good cheer; it is I; do not be afraid!"

I bore you on eagles' wings and brought you to Myself. (Exodus 19:4)

He found him a desert land, and in the howling waste of a wilderness; He encircled him, He cared for him, He guarded him as the pupil of His eye. Like an eagle that stirs up its nest, that hovers over its young, He spread His wings and caught them, He carried them on His pinions. (Deuteronomy 32:10-11)

We don't know when or how His help will come. What He wants from us is unwavering trust so we can accept and say, "Not my will, but Thine be done" (Luke 22:42). We can then marvel at the peace that comes from the Prince of peace—our Shiloh, our Messiah, our Savior. Can you ever give anyone else your junk, your trash, and receive immediate treasure? Like John, the beloved, let's learn to lean. Even if it is in the desert of our experience or the steep pathways of the unknown, we can ask Him, "Let us hear Your voice, for Your voice is sweet, and Your appearance is lovely" (Song of Solomon 2:14). There in His presence we can unload the burden and be refreshed with blessing.

THIS IS THE
DAY
THAT THE
LORD
HAS MADE
R·E·J·O·I·C·E·
A·N·D·B·E·G·L·A·D·I·N·I·T·

Chapter Six

The Son Will Shine on You

This Is the Day

This is the Lord's doing; it is marvelous in our eyes. This is the day the Lord has made; we will rejoice and be glad in it. (Psalm 118:23-24)

These two verses have emerged more and more strongly as our life verses. We chose them when we read them together on that certain day that Jay asked me to be his wife. Especially verse 24, we have quoted it, sung it, said it to each other, written it out in calligraphy, and all styles of print. We've painted it, framed it, hung it up, and prayed with it in our hearts and minds hundreds of times. It is a Word that the Lord will not allow out of our thoughts. In a way, we have hung them on the cortex of our brain. When we struggle with various trials and God says, "Do not fear," we say to each other, "This is the Day the Lord has made, we will rejoice and be glad in it."

Just to be sure we knew that God was in all of this life with us, it happened that on our first visit to the Fellowship in New York, where we planned to associate, they sang right at the beginning of the service, "This is the Day that the Lord has made." Of course, it went right to our hearts as our eyes met. *Thank You, Father.*

The words, "This is the Day" are a reminder of commitment and of faithfulness. God is always faithful to us. The question is, "Are we always faithful to Him?" Can we rejoice when the bad news strikes us down and we turn to God, as in "What now, God?" Can we rejoice in even the toughest of trials? Well, there was bad news about Robert, but was it all bad? No, it wasn't. God didn't leave us without a sustaining comfort, without hope. Yes, we wanted Bob here. Even in grieving and hurting, we could thank God even at that moment, that he was with Jesus. That is exactly why Shiona could keep saying over and over, "Robert is with Jesus." The next thought was we will be together again because we have a lively hope.

We all admit that it is easy to rejoice when the promotion comes, and children grow up respecting their parents, loving their brothers and sisters, graduating, and getting married. These are the days we happily and thankfully celebrate. There is the special thanks we have in their growth in loving and serving the same Lord and Savior. But let's be sure we know that the inconveniences, large or small, even the seeming contradictions, are not out of God's hands. Sometimes we want to take a short detour with fist banging the table just to say, "Lord, I can't handle this, I am not prepared for this!" I did this when the first diagnosis came about Shiona.

On the other hand, thinking about the fresh grave where Robert was buried, that was not a time to place a sign that says, "This is the Lord's doing, this is marvelous in our eyes." As Christians, our sorrow is not like those who do not believe. We have a living hope that is anchored firmly in the solid rock, Christ Jesus. We know that the passage altogether refers first and foremost to the promised Messiah. Nevertheless, all Scripture is given for us, for our learning. With our firm trust in our Heavenly Father and His Son, we will receive the strength to endure the test and trial of our faith. He allowed it all or He planned it all. Nothing is out of His control. He wants us to assimilate more and more that we belong to Him and He belongs to us, that we live in Him and He lives in us, that we are here for His purpose and His purposes will be accomplished in all things.

Hudson Taylor (founder of China Inland Mission in 19th century) was brought very low when he was avalanched with telegrams telling him of the CIM missionaries who were being martyred during the Boxer Rebellion. This went on day after day until finally he had this to say to his supporters back in England, "I cannot think, I cannot talk, I can hardly pray, but I can trust." That is a very low point to come to, but if we *can* say, "I can trust You" we have not bottomed out; our Father knows. We read about the early Church, the persecution was responsible for the spread of the Good News, and so also Taylor found that he had more and more candidates for mission work and the Chinese people were responding to the Gospel in greater numbers than he ever imagined. Even so, for a time or season we ache more than we can express in words.

Therefore, do not throw away your confidence, which has a great reward. For you have need of endurance, so that when you have done the will of God, you may receive what was promised. (Hebrews 10:35-36)

Whenever I read this verse, I recall sitting on the edge of Shiona's bed. It was the first time she had a seizure and only a month after her head injury. I was alarmed; Jay was trying to get a doctor. My Bible was open to this passage and as I read it I felt anchored. Since that day, it has often been a great comfort and encouragement to me.

It is good to remind ourselves that our God is the God of ALL THINGS (emphasis added by author):

Romans 8:28 says, "We know that God causes ALL THINGS to work together for good to those who love God."

Romans 8:37 says, "But in ALL these THINGS we over-whelmingly conquer through Him who loved us."

2 Corinthians 5:17 says, "Behold ALL THINGS are become new."

Philippians 4:13 says, "I can do ALL THINGS through Him who strengthens me."

Colossians 1:17 says, "He is before ALL THINGS and by Him ALL THINGS exist."

Matthew 19:26 says, " With God ALL THINGS are possible."

1 Peter 4:11 says, "In ALL THINGS God may be glorified through Jesus Christ."

Hebrews 1:2 says, "In His Son, whom He appointed heir of ALL THINGS."

Hebrews 1:3 says, "He. . . upholds ALL THINGS by the word of His power."

Hebrews 2:8 says, "Thou hast put ALL THINGS in subjection under His feet."

Romans 11:36 says, "For from Him and through Him and to Him are ALL THINGS."

Hebrews 3:4 says, "The builder of ALL THINGS is God."

Psalms 57:2-3 says, "God. . . accomplishes ALL THINGS for me."

1 Corinthians 13:4, 7 says, "Love. . . bears ALL THINGS, believes ALL THINGS, hopes ALL THINGS, endures ALL THINGS."

2 Corinthians 9:8 says, "God is able to make ALL grace abound to you, so that having ALL sufficiency in ALL THINGS at ALL times, you may abound in every good work."

Revelations 21:7 says, "He that overcomes shall inherit ALL THINGS, and I will be his God and he shall be my son." (KJV)

While writing this I am reminded of a long ago hymn by Joseph Hart:

"How good is the God we adore,
Our faithful, unchangeable Friend,
Whose love is as great as His power
And knows neither measure nor end."

*   *   *   *   *

Shut Out - Shut In

They looked for Him,
They watched for Him,
They waited along the way.
"How blessed who wait for Him," they say.

Shut out the clutter,
The thoughts, the words,
The busyness of the day.
A moment or two will clear the way.

Come, see a Man, human and divine.
Hear His voice, feel His touch.
Behold, the Man, the Son,
Only begotten of the Father.

Our beloved, Lord, Jesus Christ,
He has been waiting. . .He comes;
Close the door. Shut in with Him.
Waiting now for Thy loving-kindness, Lord!

And when the doors were shut. . . .Jesus came. . . and said, "Peace be with you!" (John 20:19)

Come, my people, enter into your rooms, and close Your doors behind you. Hide for a little moment until the indignation passes over. (Isaiah 26:20)

How blessed are all those who wait for Him. (Isaiah 30:18)

*　*　*　*　*

Early Edge of Morn

At the early edge of morn
With Christ, in quietness and calm,
In stillness or in prayer,
Or meditation on a Psalm;
Wait, and watch and listen,
Wait, and watch and listen,
Wait, and watch and listen,
At the early edge of morn.

At the early edge of morn
He'll lift from you all shame.
He will listen, He will hold you,
And He'll call you by your name.
As He waits to sit beside you,
As He waits to sit beside you,
As He waits to sit beside you,
As the joyous edge of morn.

At the early edge of morn
With the Book of books in hand,
And your heart bowed down in worship
In His truth now take your stand.

In peace and trust now resting,
In peace and trust now resting,
In peace and trust now resting
Comes the dew at early morn.

O, that early edge of morn
When the birds wake up to sing;
When the storm has rumbled on
And the gloom has taken wing;
Lingering comfort fills my soul.
Lingering comfort fills my soul.
Prompts my spirit now to sing -
Hallelujah! Hallelujah!
On this glorious edge of morn.

Give ear to my words, O Lord, consider my meditation.
Hearken unto the voice of my cry, my King, and my God:
For unto Thee will I pray. My voice shalt Thou hear in
the morning, O Lord, in the morning will I direct my
prayer unto Thee and will look up. (Psalm 5:1-3 KJV)

*   *   *   *   *

Long and Lonely Days

Do not despise the long and lonely days. We all have
them, but we must learn how to use them. Think of them as
the quiet hours you have longed for, making them days for
repentance, days of forgiveness; even restoration. They can
be days when the rough edges are soothed away by the touch
of the Potter's Hand.

Being quiet before the Lord, being humble before His
throne, being fully yielded under His Hand of grace becomes
a place for receiving. Don't resist and wonder why, just be
quiet and listen because He longs to teach you His ways that

113

you may walk with firm steps in His paths. He will teach you how to carry your cross, lest you lay it down making it a cause to stumble. Here is a refreshing word from the One who loves us with unlimited love!

The Lord your God is in the midst of you, a mighty One, a Savior — Who saves! He will rejoice over you with joy; He will rest (in silent satisfaction) and in His love He will be silent (and make no mention of past sins, or even recall them): He will exult over you with singing. (Zephaniah 3:17 AMP)

They looked to Him and were radiant. (Psalm 34:5)

Lean ever harder when the road is rough
Lean ever harder when the moment is tough
Stay on the path of the tried and the true —
"Behind and before, I will never leave you!"
"When you shine in the dark, you help others get through!"
Keep smiling and the Son will shine on you!

Shiona

Chapter Seven

Joy Unspeakable

On to the Heights

Do the days seem long and shattered,
Shattered with feelings good and bad?
Stop, lay aside all this confusion;
In making excuses, don't be flattered...

For self is on the rise again,
As pride lifts up its ugly head.
An enemy would like to see you spurn
The grace that's offered at the Throne.

Humbly bow, there's far more Treasure:
All that comes is from God's Hand.
For me He makes all grace abound
When I look up and not around.

If you then be risen with Christ,
Set your heart on things above.
For there, sits Christ upon His throne
Where your life is hidden in His great love.

God is able to make all grace abound to you, that always having all sufficiency in everything, you may have abundance for every good deed. (2 Corinthians 9:8)

If then you have been raised up with Christ, keep seeking the things above, where Christ is, seated at the right hand of God. Set your mind on the things above, not on the things that are on earth. For you have died and your life is hidden with Christ in God. (Colossians 3:1-3)

* * * * *

He Knows the Way

Stepping stone or stumbling block. In loneliness it can be either. I talked to Him about this.

I said to Him, "Jesus, I am feeling all alone - help me!"

"I have trodden the winepress alone; and from the people there was no man with Me. Is the servant above his master? You know I will never leave you nor forsake you. This is a charge I have laid on Myself," was His answer.

"Jesus, I would be Your disciple," I answered.

"I looked and there was no one to help, I was astonished and there was no one to uphold!" Jesus replied.

"Jesus, is there no helping hand?" I questioned.

"I bore the loneliness for you," He said. "I am the Helping Hand! Do not fear, for I am with you. Do not look anxiously about you, do not be uneasy, for I am your God, I will strengthen you, surely I will help you, surely I will uphold you with My righteous right hand!"

To those who do not want to believe, He is a stumbling block. By listening to Him, we find the stepping-stone to righteousness (taken from Isaiah 41:10; 63:5; Psalm 91:11; Matthew 10:24; Hebrews 13:5).

Are we smooth stones or rough edges? We have to take a look at ourselves in the mirror of the Word. Smooth stones are stones from the riverbed; made smooth by the washing of the Word. Have you been to the river or the beach and picked up the smooth, glossy stones that have tumbled about in the water for years and years? Beautiful, aren't they? The colors glow from the inside; some are translucent and reflect the light. They are shiny and smooth to the touch. The touch of the Master with His Word can make us into people who are compassionate, peaceful, and full of love for one another. He can even make us transparent because there is no more need to hide and no more rough edges because He is busy making the rough, sharp edges smooth!

Now you have become living building-stones for God's use in building His house. (1Peter 2:5 TLB)

He wants us to bring peace and harmony to the place of His choosing. This brings to mind a chorus we like to sing:

I delight to do Thy will, O Lord,
I delight to do Thy will.
And to walk with Thee is not grievous unto me,
For I delight to do Thy will.
(Psalm 40:8; 1 John 5:13)

When we choose to say, "Thy will be done," then we are letting Him choose for us. David Livingstone put it this way, "When His will is my will, then His joy is my joy!" An interesting note about David Livingstone, he was on his knees in prayer when he went to be with Jesus forever!

Come, let us go up to the mountain of the Lord. To the house of the God of Jacob; that He may teach us concerning His ways, and that we may walk in His paths. (Isaiah 2:3)

Let us keep on until we know that we know and until we always go to Him who gives the peace, the grace, the strength, assurance, and rest. He will be sure that we begin to learn from Him to serve, to be humble, patient, and the harder ones—to wait and let go. In all of this we learn that the treasure we seek is His face. When we can see His face, then we can "count it all joy!" (James 1:2 TLB). We are finally receiving from Him, "for it is God who is at work in us both to will and to do for His good pleasure" (Philippians 2:13). He and He only, will direct and make the pathway plain. His is the awesome responsibility to provide.

He knows the way that I take. (Job 23:10)

When my spirit grows faint within me, it is You who knows my way. (Psalm 142:3)

Though I walk in the midst of trouble, You preserve my life. (Psalm 138:7)

For all my ways are before You. (Psalm 119:16)

The path of the just is as a shining light, that shines more and more unto the perfect Day. (Proverbs 4:18).

Dear Heavenly Father,
  Since from forever past You have known me, my life and my way through life. Let me not stumble on the roughness or steep slopes in the pathway. Be my refuge, be my strength, and my courage. Dear Father, make provision. Wait! You have made provision! Oh, let my heart grasp You and let go of all else! Be the Quiet and Secret Place of my renewing.

Remind me by Your Holy Spirit that under Your Wings I can
always find refuge.

Thank You, Father, forever!

Tossed About

Sometimes I feel like driftwood,
Tossed upon a lonely shore.
The sea is rough, the waves so high;
My thoughts - they tumble evermore.

Give me again Thy presence calm.
Be to me my constant Friend.
Take me through these stormy waters;
Be Guide and Savior to the end.

Holy Light, shine on the path
Chosen of Thy good pleasure,
To work and will and leave all else:
There's no other path to Treasure.

And I will give you the treasure of darkness, and hidden
wealth of secret places, in order that you may know that
it is I, the Lord, the God of Israel, who calls you by your
name. (Isaiah 45:3)

I am reminded to be content because He says, "My grace
is sufficient for you" (1 Corinthians 12:9). I will need the
Helper for what lies ahead; this is not something I can do
all alone. I am sure we all have sung Elizabeth Clephane's
words many times:

"Content to let the world go by
To know no gain or loss.

My only shame my sinful self
My glory all the cross."

I am well content with weaknesses, with insults, with distresses, with persecutions, with difficulties, for Christ's sake. When weak, I am strong. (2 Corinthians 12:9-10)

Be content with what you have. (Hebrews 13:5)

Godliness with contentment is great gain. (1 Timothy 6:6)

I have learned to be content in whatever circumstances I am. I know how to get along with humble means and. . . in prosperity, any and every circumstance. . . being filled or going hungry, both of having abundance and suffering need. I can do all things through Him who strengthens me. (Philippians 4:11-12)

*   *   *   *   *

Treasure in Your Bundle

Without accepting and holding on solidly to the belief in God's sovereignty, life would be very shaky indeed. Have you ever heard someone in agony say, "I'm falling apart"? Yes, life without strong trust in Jesus can certainly cause someone to say those words of helplessness and hopelessness. But we don't need to live like we're falling over the cliff. That is why I refer to life as a bundle. It is also why I like this verse in 1 Samuel 25:29, "Should anyone rise up to pursue you and to seek your life, then the life of my lord (speaking of David) shall be bound in the bundle of the living with the Lord your God; but the lives of your enemies He will sling out as from the hollow of a sling."

A bundle is a number of things bound together, wrapped up in a package. It is what we are born with; our whole life is a gift from the Father above. He made up the bundle, He wrapped it, and then He placed you in your parents' lap. It is a package that is slowly unwrapped as we live day by day. There are surprises, treasures, trials, triumphs, and victories.

Early on we discover we are individuals and have power. We can say "yes and no" and, in one case, find smiles and hugs and, on the other hand, scowls and reprimands. We have the power to create a happy atmosphere or chaos and fistfights with lots of discipline. Even though we have power, we find out soon enough that we need something else. We need insight. We need to meet the One who made us. We need to be changed. A new heart is what we need. We bow before Him and we receive that new heart. Then one day we read, "I know the plans I have for you, plans for good and not evil to give you a future and a hope" (Jeremiah 29:11). Is that God talking to *me*? Yes, it is, and He means what He says. Let's see how it works out in an old story.

Genesis 42 and 43 tell the story of Joseph's brothers who went down to Egypt to get food because of the severe famine in the land where they lived. Joseph's brothers had not been kind to him. In fact, they had been very cruel. Because of their treatment of him, he had been sold as a slave, lied about, accused, put in prison, forgotten, lived out his life in Egypt, and was considered dead by his family. What a mean list of indignities for a young person to live with! His father wanted to die because Joseph was his favorite. But God had a plan, and God's purpose would not be thwarted. In fact, it is probably true that in this story for the first time in the Bible we see in action what Paul tells us in Romans 8:28, "And we know that God causes all things to work together for good to those who love God, to those who are called according to His purpose."

It so happened that in Israel there was desperation because of this famine. Jacob, the sorrowful, grieving father of these twelve sons, sent ten of his sons to Egypt for a supply of grain to feed his large family. They went, they paid and left shortly with sacks of grain, but they didn't know what else came with the bundles for which they were so thankful. They didn't know that God's plan for their brother Joseph was for him to be second in command in Egypt. They didn't know that God sent Joseph to Egypt to save a multitude of people from starvation. That was all in Joseph's "life bundle" and one of God's secrets. The brothers didn't know the "inside story" so they went just looking forward to bringing home food to feed the family.

There were surprises in store for them. Stopping probably for a night's rest, they looked in their sacks. That's when they found out that the money which they used to pay for this food was put back into their sacks. They were not happy or excited. They did not consider it "treasure." They were thinking, *What's going to happen to us now?* Fear paralyzes. They couldn't get passed the thought of: *We're in trouble, we will be punished, no good is going to come of this, will life ever be right again? What will our father say? When will it all end?* All these are very agonizing thoughts. We could be thinking some of these thoughts if we have some mysterious dilemma come into our lives.

Their journey into Egypt meant food for the family. That's all they had on their minds. The food was good; they needed to feed their wives, children, and their aging father. It was what came along with the food that threw them into a tailspin. It was something they knew didn't belong to them. They were afraid, very afraid. "We will be accused of stealing, we will be punished. Oh, what shall we do? This is not good." Twisted confessions and outright lies have a way of clinging to us. Something was eating at them, like when Jesus is trying to get our attention. There was only one thing to do. Go back and plead for their lives. So biting their nails and tearing their hair, they made a "U turn." Sometimes it is good to make a U turn in life!

Joseph's servant met them as they shook and groaned, and said to them, "Be at peace, your God has given you treasure in your sacks!" (Genesis 43:23). I really don't think they were ready to believe this. They had been anticipating slavery or imprisonment. This treasure in their sacks, and treasure it surely was, scared them. These strong, cruel men were uneasy and frightened.

Many times when we come against something, we beg and pray to God to remove or alter and heal the sickness, distress or the uncomfortable situation. Slowly He helps us live through the unwanted, when the unwanted does not look like treasure. Little by little, as we let Him, God gives us strength to humble ourselves, strength to help in the situation no matter how disturbing or lengthy. Why? He is showing us some of the treasures that lie enfolded in the bundle. Can you hear God whisper, "Be at peace, I have given you treasure in this bundle!"

"It is not *my* strength, it is not *my* patience, it is not in *my* ability to deal with this," we say. We finally get down on our knees in humility, asking forgiveness and say, "It is You, Lord. You have helped me. You have sustained me through this trial." That is when we begin to see that there is treasure to be had in our own personal bundle called life. Through it the Lord has grown us up a little in our faith and trust in Him. The secret? *He* is the Treasure. You see, now you know Him better. This what He wants. A child who will come to Him and say, "I can't do this by myself, Abba Father, please help me."

But Joseph's brothers are still uneasy, "It does not seem to be treasure to us!" The real treasure was yet to be unfolded to them. But they didn't know that. All they knew was fear. They were in a sense trapped, as in, "We can't handle this." However, God had a plan, a good plan. Joseph was back in their life, but they didn't know that yet either. God was working on them, an inward working. Maybe that is why they felt so uncomfortable. They had done evil and God knew it, but He loved them. They were in His plan and purpose. God was at work, and at times that can be painful, perhaps very painful.

But (for Joseph's brothers and for us) *God demonstrates His own love toward us, in that while we were yet sinners, Christ died for us.* (Romans 5:8)

They had a long spiritual journey ahead of them. They had made a long journey, but this was to be a different kind; a journey into their past actions and attitudes. The money in their sacks was an enticement to get to the real issue. It might take a while but God would not let go. He would accomplish His purpose. Joseph didn't reveal himself to them until they were ready. Their consciences were being worked on. God needed for them to admit what they had done in their past deeds to their brother. They needed to repent, to acknowledge their sins, and then in humility face their brother when he revealed himself to them. This is never easy. When this was accomplished then came the forgiveness and reconciliation.

Joseph said to them, 'Do not be afraid for am I in God's place (to judge and punish)*? And as for you, you meant evil against me, but God meant it for good in order to bring about this present result to preserve many people alive.* (Genesis 50:19-20)

Now they had their brother back and he had them. The real treasure in their sacks was confession, forgiveness, and reconciliation. Joseph urged them to bring their father, Jacob, their wives and children, all their cattle, and belongings to live in Goshen near Joseph. The last words of Joseph that we read are, "Do not be afraid, I will provide for you and your little ones." So he comforted them and spoke kindly to them (Genesis 50:21). You can read the entire beautiful story in Genesis 37 through 50. Yes, after everything, Joseph spoke kindly to them!

*　　*　　*　　*　　*

It was a few months after Robert died that we discovered friends we had known in Portland also lived now in New York only a few hours away. It wouldn't be difficult to get together from time to time. One of those visits was our turn to go to Elmira where they lived. They had recently welcomed their firstborn; that bundle of new life was accompanied with Down's syndrome. We empathized and together spoke often about God and His ways with us, and the unexpected challenges He entrusts to us. We knew each other well and felt a common bond of "buying the field to own the treasure." On this particular visit of ours, they wanted to take us to see the "Glory Hole."

"What is the Glory Hole?" we wanted to know.

"Oh, you'll see!" they weren't about to tell us ahead of time.

They drove us to the Steuben Art Gallery where the glass blowing artists did their work. We found seats in the balcony overlooking about six huge furnaces. Above the opening of each furnace was a sign in very large letters: GLORY HOLE. Each GLORY HOLE was glowing immensely as the furnaces radiated extreme heat. We looked at each other and little by little the message dawned on us. Our friends knew already as they waited for the message to register with us. The Glory Hole could that be synonymous with "Furnace of Affliction" (Isaiah 48:10).

No way did a spectator want to go close and get a good look. Neither do many want to get close when there is such heavy sorrow and grief nearby. We didn't either when we heard the news about Robert or later the diagnosis for Shiona. Our friends were not overjoyed with the diagnosis which came with their little one. Their situation would mean challenges ahead unexpected, of course. For us also, but a different set of challenges. We sat there looking at each other with that knowing look which said, "Yes, we have experienced the Glory Hole."

The Glory Hole at the Steuben Art Gallery produces beautiful, expensive glass artifacts, but only by each piece being immersed into that place of fiery trial heated to some 2000 degrees F. The artist-craftsman, holding the long pole with molten glass at the tip, carefully watches the amount of exposure and which twist or turn will bring out the beauty he desires in this one unique piece. Our visit to the Steuben Art Gallery was a vivid lesson to us. Why, though, were we all there sitting in that Gallery watching misery, at times holding our breath? Of course there was only one reason; we all were anticipating the exquisite outcome!

To own the Treasure we must embrace the Bundle. Saying it another way, buy the field to own the treasure (Matthew 13:44). It can also be likened to the oyster embracing the grain of sand, *loving* it with nacre until a precious pearl is formed. Pressure and heat are used deep in the earth to form the diamonds, emeralds, and rubies. But we are real people; we feel things, we hurt, we feel isolated, and alone. Yet God does not leave us alone. He is there with us and as the bundle of our life is unfolded. We need to remember that we embrace the whole bundle to receive the blessing. It is one of God's ways of shaping and making us into the image of His dear Son. Again and again I am reminded: Embrace whatever God has given, it is the only way to blessing.

As I walked around that certain park in our city, this was the lesson He was teaching me. It was not accomplished in a day or so, I can't even remember how long. Jay and I were faced with the difficult dilemma that came with Shiona's life. We didn't know what to do with it. This brain injury and the subsequent issues which arose from it puzzled the doctors and us.

Early on we really thought that her health needs would shortly be unraveled. But God knew that we needed Him foremost. Although it is true that we have seen some things slowly improve, other difficulties remain, and even more, some areas became greater challenges. But God, our Father, is in it all with us, working in each of our lives, including Shiona's. She came as a very special gift from our Heavenly Father, and that fact does not change.

We rejoiced when she was born. We didn't see everything that was to be unfolded in this our "bundle of joy." But as life unrolled we started saying things like, "Why, God?" "How long?" Little by little He began to reveal treasure as the challenge increased. With His wisdom we have found that *He* is the Treasure. Our part is to humbly yield to His will and His plan. We had to embrace the work that He planned for us to undertake. We have to continue asking for His strength and His patience. In all of this we have found that *He is the Treasure* in our Bundle. He is the Peace, the Comfort, the Encourager, the Strength; and our Hope in the glorious future is in Him.

Christ in you the hope of Glory. (Colossians 1:27)

Dear Father, open our eyes and hearts further to receive what You have for us, and to accept the trial, to carry the load, to walk the steep road. We will count it all joy, we will receive the victory, for we are called to receive blessing.

Help us in this You have asked us to do. I pray in the Name of Your Son, Jesus. Amen.

> *For My thoughts are not your thoughts, neither are your ways My ways, declares the Lord. For as the heavens are higher than the earth, so are My ways higher than your ways and My thoughts than your thoughts.* (Isaiah 55:8-9)

Our friends who took us to the Glory Hole have reminded us of this Word many times. It is the Word that continues to sustain them, too.

The following hymn from Caroline S. Berg is one that has been a safeguard and help to maintain my confidence on this long journey. The words and thoughts have long been a comfort to me. For this reason I include it here for you.

> *Day by day and with each passing moment,*
> *Strength I find to meet my trials here*
> *Trusting in my Father's wise bestowment,*
> *I've no cause for worry or for fear.*
> *He whose heart is kind beyond all measure*
> *Gives unto each day what He deems best*
> *Lovingly, its part of pain and pleasure,*
> *Mingling toil with peace and rest.*

> *Ev'ry day the Lord Himself is near me*
> *With a special mercy for each hour;*
> *All my care He fain would bear, and cheer me,*
> *He whose name is Counsellor and Pow'r.*
> *The protection of His child and treasure*
> *Is a charge that on Himself He laid*
> *"As your days, your strength shall be in measure,"*
> *This the pledge to me He made.*

Promises. medabrim.org.il.

" .israel@gmail.com.

Help me then in ev'ry tribulation
So to trust Your promises, O Lord,
That I lose not faith's sweet consolation
Offered me within Your Holy Word.
Help me, Lord, when toil and trouble meeting,
E'er to take, as from a father's hand,
One by one, the days, the moments fleeting,
Till I reach the promised land.

* * * * *

Treasure Trove

Jesus tells of a man who discovered treasure in a field. In his excitement he sold everything he owned to get enough money to buy the field and get the treasure, too (see Matthew 13:44). This scripture was my meditation on daily walks around the park. Was He talking to me about buying a field? Could the dilemma in my life be likened to the field? Was He saying I would find treasure in this my dilemma? Could I whole-heartedly give myself to this new way? The dilemma I was facing meant hard work; weekly, monthly, yearly, perhaps life-long. I hesitated putting my shoulder to the task and situation which indicated it would not be easy!

Yet, it seemed that He was saying,
"Accept the assignment."
"Embrace the task."
"Bear reproach,"
"Even many obstacles."
"Be misunderstood, it matters not."
"Let your life take a different path."
"There is treasure to be had."

So I asked the Lord to help me
In giving up the fight,
To surrender all the struggling thoughts
And to walk in my Father's might.

The assignment I accepted
And in my heart I prayed,
"Help me, Lord, Oh, help me
To embrace this heavy task;
This bundle to surround with love;
And wait for treasure trove."

Years have followed on and on;
Yet He is always there.
I saw, and now I know it's true.
I heard, and it is real!
Treasure is hidden in this precious bundle,
At times a heavy burden,
Often laced with deepening care.

Come, reap a harvest of His treasures,
As He guides with lamp along the road.
Be welcomed daily in His courts,
Meet with the tender Lamb of God.

He lifts the somber sadness
That threatens darkness on many days.
For gracious and merciful is the Lord.
And kind in all His ways.

Stories of mercy remain fresh in mind,
Yet I was often caught in despair.
But my wavering faith held firmly fast,
By His comfort, surprise, and His care.

His acts are awesome, loving and kind,
His goodness, abundant, not spare.
His power and glory are often shown
In His guidance and peace not rare.

His wisdom and patience are never lean,
He is Fortress, Shield, Defender, and Friend.
To His strong tower; Oh, how oft have I run;
"Come, weary heart, take of My strength again!"

So. . .
If the Father comes to meet you,
With a special one to keep,
Just remember that He loves you -
Do not fret, though you may weep.

God has given you a bundle,
And a blessing you'd rather have?
Embrace the bundle; hold it tight,
For there's treasure, just out of sight.

Faith will tug against the feelings:
Are you not called to this your duty?
Faith says, "Strengthen the feeble knee,
Look to Christ who holds the key."

For many treasures lie enfolded,
In the trial of our faith.
But our Lord still longs to give us
Strength and patience, peace, and grace.

"Be at ease, do not be afraid. . .
Your God has given you treasure" (Genesis 43:23).

133

Just remember...
Holy and awesome is His name.
And by His blood He overcame.
Faith will triumph, as He planned.
Daily we are in His hand.
Always above us flies His banner;
Always unfurled is His Love.

WATCH OVER YOUR
heart with all
diligence, FOR OUT
OF it are the issues
OF LIFE   Prov 4:23

Chapter Eight

Guard Your Heart

Tuesday's Psalm

I held onto anger as a garment,
How uncomfortable it was, but on I went...
Quickly, avoiding the thought to pray.

It was of my own making,
The disappointment of that day.
But Lord, You stood waiting, waiting.
You Lord, were guiding, guiding.
It was I who disobeyed.
It was my folly, my choice, my making...
This folly to disobey.

So I took an offense
And wore it like a garment;
And clearly lost my way.
It was Your guidance, Lord,
When first I made the plan,
But, I gave in and failed again.

Now I wore an overcoat,
Add hat, gloves, and scarf thereto.
Incognito, silent; none can reach me now.

It's hard to shed those garments,
Even when it's warm outside.
For the cold is in my heart,
Where garments make no warmth.

Lord, help me break the silence
And run to You again.
Help me shed this silent shroud,
Oh, how foolish I have been.
Please, help me, Lord. I'm dying
'Neath this heavy weight of sin.

Un-spin this web of sin.
Clothe me once again
In garments of Salvation. . .
In Your own righteousness.

Oh, that my ways were steadfast in obeying Your decrees!
Then I would not be put to shame when I consider all
Your commands. (Psalm 119:5-6)

Boundaries

Have you ever felt full of worry and perplexity, trying to push away that hemmed-in feeling? We know this is not God's Way! But we do it. This is not Faith—it is arguing with our Heavenly Father. It is not "waiting on God," it is not patiently "resting," and it's not "leaning on Jesus' breast" as John did. It is allowing harassment and unsettledness to disturb our place of peace. It is playing the Martha/Mary game of fussing or feasting, resisting or resting. We waddle back and forth from worship to worry and back again, when we should be resting and rejoicing since He is beside His own. Can we not look beyond and above, and live within the borders of peace?

Amy Carmichael speaks in one of her books in a picture-perfect way as she describes the fields in Ireland bordered with rough gray stones. This reminds me of borders that I am all too familiar with: the borders or boundaries in my life. Sometimes they do take on a rough, gray look as I take my own way, relying on my own feeble resources. But are they meant to be so? Take a look and see what God says about our borders in Isaiah 54:12, "I will make. . . all thy borders of pleasant stones." In other translations it says, "even stones of delight,(Rotherham) precious stones, and sparkling jewels (NIV). Indeed, Psalms 147:14 tells me He makes our border peace. Now I need to learn how to transform my thinking of rough gray borders to the beautiful pictures told by God.

Without our heavenly Father's watch-care over us, how much misery and chaos would confront us? In His wisdom He places the borders. Since He does place the borders, we can with certainty, believe that they will be truly beautiful, pleasant, and peaceful. Does He not live with us inside the borders, in our very lives? When we look up and not around, when we fix, fasten, attach, secure firmly, and set permanently our eyes on Jesus (Hebrews 12:2 AMP), we know His nearness, and His closeness in every kind of way. His closeness is always close-enough. However, often in my struggle I allow the uncomfortable circumstances that surround me to enclose and threaten me. I see these as barricades to my spirit, and the communion with my Heavenly Father is all too distant. I have lost perspective and focus; anger wants to arise and I begin to smolder. Then I pray, "Lord Jesus, lift my eyes; *help me* to lift my eyes. Sustain me in this troubling moment, cause me to remember the 'more thans.' First, of loving You foremost (Matthew 10:47); second, the 'more than' of Your grace and gladness (Psalm 4:7); thirdly, the 'more than' of conquering" (Romans 8:37). Then it happens, like the ladies in Mark 16:4, "looking up, they see the stone rolled away." I hope you have had such a "come quickly, Lord Jesus" when the Holy Spirit comes and you experience a lifting up and a looking up to see the forbidding "stone" has been rolled away.

Perhaps if we take a look at how He sees the borders, we won't be so prone to climb and stumble our way through the next disturbing circumstance, whether it's illness, loneliness, or a long walk with no end in sight. Let's try to see them as borders of protection, borders of safety, borders of peace and comfort. They are borders to prevent loss or deterioration in our life, and to recover communion with Him as we re-establish our focus.

After all, what God is doing is much more than we can see. Isn't this the promise that He is molding us to the image of His Son? Do we slide into these pleasant places easily? No, we don't, but we have the Helper, the Comforter. Boundaries are disciplines, learning points, and often cause growing pains. Paul also called these things the fellowship of His suffering (Philippians 3:10), reminding us to make our life an offering. It is our privilege to suffer with our Savior. What a comfortable feeling are those pleasant stones now to me. Think of the preciousness of borders because He builds them. They can guide us to an increased and better knowing of our heavenly Father and His Son Jesus, our Source of godly riches. Yes! Lovely borders, indeed!

A memory comes to mind of one small moment on the way to the doctor's office with my seven year old sitting beside me in the car. Unaware of my concern, my worried thoughts about the results of recent tests she had undergone, she began singing the scripture chorus from Psalm 3:3-4.

My glory and the lifter of my head.
My glory and the lifter of my head.
For Thou, O Lord, art a shield to me,
My glory and the lifter of my head.
I cried unto the Lord with my voice
I cried unto the Lord with my voice
I cried unto the Lord with my voice,
And He heard me out of His holy hill.

I wish you could have heard her sing it! As she sang this over and over it gradually became easy for me to sing along. Shiona didn't know I needed this, but the Comforter did! He'd heard my inward cry and He came. Through Shiona's clear lovely voice He came at that very moment and lifted my head, using my little girl, unaware, and broke up the wearying thoughts. So my inward eyes went upward as God strengthened me, and I felt ever so encouraged by the reminder. The boundary in our life of her medical situation became peaceful again, and the memory now has become a precious jewel to me. Jesus *is truly* our Peace!

The Hand of our God is upon all them for good who seek Him. (Ezra 8:22)

*　　*　　*　　*　　*

For Contentment and Trust

Gracious Father, the testing times are still
With me, as I contemplate this day.
And still I wait till You open the door,
Making way for things I've been anxious for.

The end result that I see my home
The way I've prepared in my mind.

But what You've been teaching me
Is of far more worth, if I calmly wait Your mind.

I'll sing a song that is born of trust
In my Father, who loves me so.
You'll teach me to love and care much more,
Oh, so much more than in lovely, and neat and clean.

If the universe can wait for the coming glory,
While You prepare the Bride for Your Son,
So I can wait as You teach my heart to find rest
In offering my best - my heart, my soul, and mind.

Forgive me, my Father, for anxious thoughts,
For furrowed brow, and rough-raveled edges,
That steal from me precious moments of joy.
This, my prayer, loving Father, please hear.

To be content, not hurried nor rude,
Nor boastful, proud nor dull,
To give ungrudging what will never become rare -
Your Love - as on Your strength I lean.

When my anxious thoughts multiply within me, Thy consolations delight my soul. (Psalm 94:19

I will not leave you comfortless, I will come to you. (John 14:18)

* * * * *

When Peace Rules

Much of late has been turmoil entrenched.
But wait, it need not be,

Let the peace of God rule in my heart,
And surely the struggle must flee!
Grant it so, dear Father.
(Colossians 3:15)

In quietness —
The quiet tongue.
In confidence —
The yielded heart
Your strength shall be.
(Isaiah 30:15)

This scripture in Isaiah was another gift from Robert as we turned pages in his Bible and journal. As I read it the Lord seemed to say, "I am speaking to you, and so has your son spoken to you." Family relationships live on, a gift from our Heavenly Father. Words spoken and later remembered touch a deep place in our hearts. Not only are we encouraged in them, but also reminded of covenant relationship; a God-given wonder. Make memories, they succor us as Robert said, "When we don't have each other's presence anytime we want."

* * * * *

Our Supreme and Sovereign God

Lord Jesus Christ
The Person of Comfort and Rest
For He encompasses everything.
As for Wisdom and Knowledge
There is no equal;
Making worry unnecessary,
And humbling the believer.

*   *   *   *

Revelation 4:11
Worthy art Thou, O Lord,
To receive glory, honor and power
For Thou hast created all things;
For Thy pleasure they were created.
Worthy art Thou, O Lord.

*   *   *   *   *

How hard it is to assimilate, "except it die. . . it abides alone" (John 12:24). Words of Jesus! We were in Elmira, New York, visiting our friends who had taken us to the Steuben Art Gallery. That same weekend we visited their church. Their Pastor preached on this passage in John. Everything he said was transferred to the recent events of Robert's home-going. At this time these words were very difficult to meditate on, but I continued to reflect on that Scripture for many years.

At the beginning of his journal, Robert wrote, "I know He (Jesus) wants my life and I have given my life to Him for any purpose that would be of His benefit." These are words that generate thanksgiving in a Christian parent's heart. But when death takes that young one, they become words to grapple with. When and how can one see the harvest spoken of when the life has been suddenly taken away? Endurance; that says it all. We don't have endurance, until our Father leads us in ways that we will learn. We learn while abiding. In John 15 Jesus talks about abiding. Speaking of Robert's family and friends, some couldn't accept it, but we chose to believe.

I have tried and chosen you in the furnace of affliction.
(Isaiah 48:10)

Then we prayed, "Let all die; our will, our desires, our preferences, and our selfishness. Let it all die, Lord, but 'do revive us according to Thy loving-kindness'" (Psalm 119:88). Slowly, with time, anxiety is no more; all is at rest, at peace in God's will, God's provision, God's mercy! It all comes, but only in His time and way.

As we look back there were times of resistance, restlessness, and sadness in regards to the happenings in the lives of both our children. Yes, we strongly desired life and health for these children that God loaned us. The bundle of life was unwrapping and we saw heartache, not treasure. But God did not give up. His Word is a treasure house, but we can't be satisfied just reading it casually, having a goal of read-the-Bible-through-each-year. It takes time to meditate, to dig, to let the Words He chooses penetrate our mind and spirit, pointing us in His direction. As we read, a strong Word confronted us, "Seek My face." We knew our hearts must respond like David's did, "Your face, O Lord, we will seek" (Psalm 27:8).

When we follow His command, that's when we find gold—promises and hope to build our life on. It is true that He changes our attitudes, our desires, and preferences. All must line up with His. Like Jeremiah who said, "Thy words were found and I ate them. And Thy words became for me a joy and the delight of my heart" (Jeremiah 15:16). Jesus who *is* the Word, said, "I am the bread of life" (John 6:35). When we truly eat and take Him in, there comes to us the strength to lift the burden, the joy to carry through, and the compassion to allow and accept the interruptions, and the limitations; even to accept His denials. When we refuse, what is left for us? Certainly there is not the blessing, present/future reward, or the peace of having our hand in His hand. What remains is only our feeble strength fighting Him and never finding peace. We know not how, but we know there is that mysteriously hidden blessing in the trial, whatever form it takes, requiring only our yielded will.

Watch over your heart with all diligence, for out of it are the issues of life. (Proverbs 4:23)

* * * * *

By nature we want to discard or fix the broken things —

The broken vessel
The broken ship
The broken candle
The broken bread
The kernel of wheat
But He says "No" —
No glory without breaking
No food without breaking
No light without the breaking
No anointing without breaking
No Savior with the breaking!

Again, we find how much higher are His thoughts than our thoughts; His ways than our ways (Isaiah 55:8-9).

"He sits as King at the flood" (Psalm 29:10), but does not stop the waters. Robert drowned: God is sovereign. *Our fleeting wish that tugs must drown in the sea of God's sovereignty!* His will must prevail.

"The Lord will accomplish what concerns her" (Psalm 138:8). But He does not heal her! Shiona is disabled: God is sovereign. *Our persistent desire must be permanently disabled in the sovereignty of God.* His will must prevail. So, we rest in His Sovereignty.

Our Sovereign Father, we are at peace, and we thank You, Father.

*   *   *   *   *

Anxious Thoughts

Fold your beating wings, you anxious thoughts,
Disturb my peace no longer.
I trust in God, my Lord, My Savior.

Centered on Him, my thoughts will ponder.
And sitting at His glorious feet,
These thoughts and prayers I oft repeat.

Oh come, Lord Jesus, to clean my mind;
So tender, yet distracted by a worldly shrine.
Yes, Heavenly Father, only You can change
My empty heart that is, oh, so vain.

The Son of God the precious Life-gift has given
That I His way might follow, no longer lonely or riven
His Love-light shines through the grit and the grim,
As He waits, my thirsting heart tuned to Him.
My eyes wait. . .
wait. . .
"Wait upon the Lord, my God" (Psalm 123:3).
On God's shoulder I lay the burdens - even heavy burdens,
And the blessing, yes, many blessings, will rest on me!

Co-authored with Shiona

Chapter Nine

Harvest Home

Harvest Home

Around the globe we share the feast
Of Christ, the Broken Bread,
The manna fell, and just enough,
To feed the hungry tribe.

The broken ones, O Lord, You loved.
You knew the cost, and yet
Some thousand years and many lambs,
The secret safely kept.

In feeding trough in Bethlehem
Is where the Christ Child lay.
He came to be our Feast Divine;
He is the Living Way.

The shepherds came by High command.
The Magi, too, rejoiced.
With gifts of love; stars bright above,
Christ's journey had just begun.

In Your design, at Your command,
We'll keep the royal feast.
You searched us out, as David did,
When Mephibosheth he found.

Now Mephi sat as David's son,
E'en orphaned, lame, alone;
At David's table freshly spread;
Embraced by kingly love.

God's loving call is for each one.
We encompass every need.
Though lonely, slow or blind or lame;
To Christ it's all the same.

Such table, Lord, You lay for us!
You bid the feast begin!
In our wonder, awe and humble faith
Your Harvest Home does us embrace.

The King's Table

When He was born Jesus was laid in a manger—a feeding trough. We think how lowly a beginning He had. But as we get to know Him, we marvel that He was willing to humble Himself, to become so lowly. We see that this lowly birth of His, even a feed trough, was pointing to His becoming the Bread of Life. He said, "I am the Bread of Life" (John 6:35). Shouldn't we believe on Him and feed on Him? The whole world is starving for bread for the body. Even after feeding them, we know there is still dissatisfaction because we know we are sinners, we are incomplete. But to satisfy that dissatisfaction is the summit of His coming.

Jesus had been teaching a long time when His disciples came to Him and said, "The place is desolate and it is already quite late; send them away so they can get something to eat." I wonder where they would have sent them. But Jesus said, "You give them something to eat!"

Don't you think they were bewildered? That didn't sound like an easy request. In fact it was quite a big order when looking out at a crowd of five thousand. They must have wondered what Jesus had in mind. Then a boy came with five loaves and two fish and gave them to Jesus. He blessed the food, broke the loaves, and kept giving portions to the disciples to set before them. They all ate and were satisfied; all five thousand, plus women and children (Matthew 14:13-21).

*   *   *   *   *

At the end of a long day, He still had *time* to feed five thousand.
To the disciples who said, "Send them away,"
it must have seemed too much.

At the end of a long day, He still had *strength*
to feed five thousand.
The disciples who said, "Send them away,"
looked at each other so wearied and worn.

At the end of a long day, He still had *compassion*
to feed five thousand.
The disciples who said, "Send them away,"
losing patience, longed only for rest.

At the end of a long day, Jesus said to the disciples,
"You feed them."
But *He* broke the bread, divided the fish,
and five thousand were amply fed.

At the end of a long day, there was still much to do:
"Go gather the fragments
That nothing be lost." With twelve baskets full, let the
lesson be learned . . . .

It may be a room full, and there may be just one,
Yet it seems too much, we're all wearied and worn.
Our patience is gone and we long for a rest,
But our Savior who's with us, hears our faint cry.
He reaches with love, and embraces us still.
He refreshes our souls, our emptiness fills.
He's our Master who says, "Come, lean on Me;
We'll toil together, none need ever be lost."

Later . . .
At the end of a long day - - - - - LOOK!
Our heart-baskets are filled . . .with thanksgiving
for our King!

With our hands lifted up,
With our mouths filled with praise,
With hearts of thanksgiving,
We bless Thee, O Lord,
We bless Thee, O Lord,
We bless Thee, O Lord,
With hearts of thanksgiving,
We bless Thee, O Lord.
(Psalm 134:2; 68:3-4)

*   *   *   *   *

Many people misunderstood Jesus on that day of the
fish and loaves. They thought, "Here is Someone who could
endlessly supply our wants." He was Someone, but they
didn't recognize Who He was. They tried to remind Jesus

that their fathers ate manna in the wilderness. But Jesus had something else in mind for them; something that would disturb their thoughts.

"Your fathers ate manna in the wilderness, and they died. He who eats My flesh and drinks My blood has eternal life; and I will raise him up on the last day. For My flesh is true food, and My blood is true drink. It is not Moses who has given you the bread out of heaven but it is My Father who gives you the true bread out of heaven. For the bread of God is that which comes down out of heaven, and gives life to the world."

They got quite excited about this and said, "Lord, evermore give us this bread." They weren't catching on yet.

Then came the shocking news, *"I am the Bread of Life. He who comes to Me shall not hunger, and he who believes in Me shall never thirst."*

The Jews grumbled about Him: "Eat my flesh and drink my blood?" To them, He was *only* the carpenter from Nazareth. (John 6:34-52).

Jesus also says to the multitude, *"Do not work for the food which perishes, but for the food which endures to eternal life, which the Son of Man shall give to you, for on Him the Father, even God, has set His seal."*

When they heard this they said to Him, *"What shall we do, that we may work the works of God?"*

Jesus answered them, *"This is the work of God, that you believe in Him whom He has sent"* (John 6:27-29).

The grumbling Jews had to hear many things that were very hard for them to digest. They wanted to remain on the same path on which they grew up. Jesus was plowing hard ground that day. He wanted them to know there is something more necessary than food for the body. Today Jesus is still plowing ground. He came to free us also from the slavery of not only pleasing others and ourselves, but of all legalism and the futility of trying to work for our salvation. But we do not come into His kingdom that way, nor do we find peace and satisfaction.

I can recall a time when this Scripture was very meaningful to me. I was trying to please others and my mind was struggling with God's will and the rules others would seek to impose on me. Jesus wants us to look in a different direction. He wants us to look to Him, to receive Him, be cleansed from sin and live eternally. Then it can be said of us, "They looked to Him and were radiant" (Psalm 34:8).

In an earlier encounter, Jesus was sitting by Jacob's well. He was tired and thirsty while waiting for the disciples who had gone to the village to find something to eat. When they returned, they marveled that He had been talking with a woman, but held their tongues. (It is interesting to note that while the Jews were harking back to Moses, this woman was pointing back to Jacob's well. We can mistakenly lean on our family history and think that God counts that history to our credit. But He doesn't, it is all about Him!) Soon the woman left with a Divine message about Living Water, but the disciples were anxious for Him to eat.

"We have food, Rabbi, eat!"

His mysterious answer to them was, "I have food to eat that you do not know about."

They wondered, "Do you think someone brought Him food?"

But Jesus was giving them something more to "chew" on. Knowing their puzzled thoughts, He said, "My food is to do the will of Him who sent Me, and to accomplish His work."

Then He instructed them about sowing and reaping, with the ultimate of rejoicing together, the joy of laboring together with other believers through prayer, support, and encouragement. This indeed is food for our souls as we learn when we come into His kingdom. Some are on the front lines doing God's work and some are the essential backup, also doing God's work. In every way God is honored (John 4:1-38).

What does all this have to do with taste and see that the Lord is good (Psalm 34:8)? Have you begun eating at the table spread for you? God invites you to His supper. You are invited to eat and drink the Son of God, for He is heavenly food, and gives Everlasting Water. It is in His Word that we are to eat the Word, as Jeremiah did when he said, "I found Your Words and I did eat them, they became the joy and rejoicing of my heart" (Jeremiah 15:16). That's how we grow up, to know what He wants of us, and what He wants us to do. Just as a child grows day by day and year by year; so must we.

Read His Word, stop and think about it, study and meditate on it, memorize it, talk about it, and sing it. Special verses or passages will stick with you and sometime later the Holy Spirit will remind you of some Words that will be significant for that particular situation facing you. You will be surprised, thankful, and awestruck as He, in His omnipotent way, will instruct you. You will be saying to others, "God is good; taste and see!"

Yet, there is another side to all this: God's side. Now we are the Bride, His Beloved and like the Bride in Song of Solomon, we say to Him, "May my beloved come into His garden and eat its choice fruits!" (Song of Solomon 4:16). For it is He who has planted after plowing the fallow ground. He has watered and fed the seed sown in the soil of our hearts. Then He comes to find pleasure and a fragrance spread abroad in this His garden. He has done all of this for His pleasure.

Can we not anticipate that He may be pleased in us? That He can find love in our hearts for Him, the ones He has created and died for? That as He looks and grieves over this whole earth He might, on this sinful planet, find pleasure for Himself? We are His beloved ones and He joys over us with singing (Zephaniah 3:17). Might we share with the laborers in the harvest fulfilling His pleasure? What a privilege, what a marvel when we think that we can be a pleasure to the King of kings! Worth repeating is Revelation 4:11.

Worthy art Thou, O Lord, to receive glory and honor and power; for Thou hast created all things, and for Thy pleasure they are and were created. (KJV)

Jesus gave us Himself so we could be born anew, receive everlasting life, and feed on Him through His Word so that we can remember Him in a very special way. We can commune with Him and fellowship with Him because when Jesus ate the Passover with His disciples, and He broke bread, He said, "This is my body which is given for you. This cup is the new covenant in My blood; do this in remembrance of Me." Before He did this with His disciples He said, "I have earnestly desired to eat this Passover with you before I suffer." He said this knowing He was on the way to the cross to be that Lamb of the Passover, and it was His desire! Let us remember to do this in remembrance of Him (Luke 22:14-20).

* * * * *

In preparing for this "Remembrance Feast" it is well to have a little talk with Jesus:

"Jesus, do I forget Thee?"
"Do I ignore Thee?"
"Yes, I am ashamed and confess,
Asking Your forgiveness, dear Savior."

When the penitent thief on the cross said to You, "Jesus, remember me when You come into Your Kingdom," You answered with an immediate promise. "Today, you will be with Me in Paradise" (Luke 23:29-43).

Would we ever need to ask You to remember us? Jesus, You are always faithful. You are never unmindful of me, or my loved ones, Your loved ones. You are steadfast, unchanging, and merciful. All we can ask is Your mercy and Your forgiveness. We ask You for the prompting of Your Holy Spirit to keep us ever mindful of You.

Remember Me", You asked Your disciples and us to remember You. Even with full knowledge of our human frailty, You disclosed Yourself to us, calling us friends; because You share Your secrets with us, knowing that we would stumble, even like Peter, we would fail. Yet, Your love, mercy, forgiveness and faithfulness are never withheld, nor would You ever condemn. You are too wonderful and we will continue to ask Your forgiveness. Let us never take the wonders of Your love for granted. May we all, always remember You. We thank You for Your Love. Amen.

*   *   *   *   *

The Holy Family

We are the Holy Family; He Himself set us apart.
We are holy through the blood of the suffering Son of God.
Help us reach and touch another as we learn to trust and love;
To share a sweet communion through His dying on the cross.

As reflections of our Savior, let our gifts be shared together.
For each will find some treasure in the life that he's been given.
Tenderly touched with our feelings, Jesus shows us
how to care;

How to gather up the weaker ones in their struggle to come near.

The struggle to be included, Jesus saw it as He walked.
On the road to Jairus' daughter, one reached His robe to touch.
Another was too short to see and so he climbed a tree,
But Jesus knew and saw Him - I wonder would have we?

Along the way there was one blind, how he longed for Jesus' touch.
With husky voice he stopped the Savior, was called right to His side.
Not needing now his shabby cloak, he was quickly gathered in.
No longer on the outside, no longer cold, alone, no longer looking in;
Now he would praise the Savior: Another heart was warmed.

Three days they despaired along the road, when Jesus found these two.
As He opened up the Word, new passion filled their hearts.
The warm enclosure of His presence to ourselves we dare not keep.
The joy comes in the giving of the invitation "Come."

Let us wait and watch and listen for the lonely, whimpering cry;
"I am cold, alone and hungry, 'twould be better if I die."
He wants them in His circle, in the circle of God's love.
So we'll unclasp our tight communion to bring the lost ones in,
And brightly light their lonely road and bring them night to day.
"And I'll be with you to the end," says the Truth, the Life, the Way.

Janet's father with his
grandkids, on their return
from Germany.

Meet the Muthmanns, just returned from
Germany; Janet, Shiona, Robert and Jay.

Shiona with
Papa Jay.

And a birthday for Shiona, sweet sixteen!

A lovely summer visit with German grandparents in Hopewell Junction, New York.

Happy graduates!
Shiona 8th grade, Robert 12th.

Looking joyfully to the future;
a Goodbye party when Shiona,
Janet and Jay had to leave Robert and
Debbie for a New York adventure.

Here's Lassie, about two
years into her friendship
with Shiona.

Shiona is so sure Grandpa needs
some German lessons!

The Wind blows where it wishes, and you hear the sound of it, but do not know where it comes from and where it is going; so is everyone who is born of the Spirit

John 3:8

Chapter Ten

Spirit Wind

Light from a Broken Candle

"Last night Jesus showed me a candle like this."
-Robert Muthmann

The day Robert showed me this picture of a broken candle, both of us were puzzled by it. When he went to Jesus, the only thing I could see in the picture was Robert died, yet the memory and the things he said and did would live on in our life as a family and in those who knew him. When Shiona's difficulties surfaced I saw her life broken in many ways, but alive in this life with us, and for Jesus. The image is also universal. As you read in "Broken and Fragmented" we are all broken coming into this world. Receiving Jesus brings us into His kingdom, but then every trial we are to count as all joy, thereby giving glory to our

Father in heaven. Best of all our light will never go out; we will shine all through eternity!

*   *   *   *   *

The Broken Candle
A Parable

Once there was a Man who was a Candle-maker. First He made molds for His candles. He made many shapes and sizes of molds. He was the designer of the molds and made them to suit His own purposes. When the molds were ready and He was satisfied with them, He set them aside until He prepared wax and wick. He carefully gathered all the material together for the wax. He needed a proper mixture heated to exactly the right temperature. While the wax was heating, He inserted into each mold a wick of certain length and thickness to give the proper flame when lit. The wax was carefully poured into the molds then set aside for cooling. The next day the candles were taken out of the molds and set up for display after finishing touches. The candles were sold and taken to various homes and places where they could give light.

However, the candles did not give light until the Flame was brought and used to ignite the wick. This was the work of the Candle-lighter. The Candle-lighter trimmed the wick of a certain candle, then lit it with the flame. He watched it for a while and saw that the flame began to flicker. The wick needed trimming. He did this. The candle wondered why, but the Candle-lighter knew what He was doing. When the wick was trimmed, the candle's flame glowed much more strongly. Again the flame flickered and almost went out, but when the Candle-lighter trimmed the wick everything was fine again. There was a strong light in the place where the candle was used, and people were helped by that candle to do their necessary work.

For a while the candle continued to burn strongly and brightly. Then one day something unexpected happened. The candle with the bright, strong flame was found to be broken, and the Candle-maker came and took it away. The flame continued to burn brightly and the Candle-maker said there was a special reason for this happening. The candle, He said, would no longer be used in the same way as other candles. But that was all right, He said, because He was the Master Candle-maker and He knew what He was doing. He said that the flame would still be bright, and that others would see by its light. The other candles missed that candle standing right there with them, but somehow they knew the light was still shining, the flame would still be bright.

The Candle-maker said, "You see, the flame still uses the wax and wick of that candle, the light still glows. How that happens to a broken candle is My secret. But now that this candle cannot stand by itself because it is broken, I will hold the candle. The candle in My hand will be used where I choose and give light in many places and in many ways that would not have been possible when it was standing in its own candlestick. I will take care of the broken candle and I will not extinguish its flame."

The Candle-maker took good care of the candle, and its flame did not go out.

The people of God shall shine as brightly as the sun's brilliance, and those who turn many to righteousness will glitter like stars forever. (Daniel 12:3)

*   *   *   *   *

This Candle Won't Light

This candle won't light! It needs trimming you say.
It's the wick, it's too proud, or the flame. What's in the way?

Give it air, give it breath; it will flare into flame.
It will glow and give light to the poor and the lame.

Sometimes it sputters, and throws off black smoke;
But the Spirit that breathes will trim it - no joke!

Burn steadily on, little flame, for the Lord.
He gives the light while you give Him your world.

And 'round you He'll turn more hearts from their shame,
They'll see His dear face and take on His Name!

*   *   *   *   *

Despair to Delight

Light of the world;
    Shine on me
        On my path
            On my work.

Ladder to Your Throne:
    Lend me Your hand
        Help me climb
            Lead me to Yourself.

Fire of God:
    Burn the depression
        The sadness
            Out of my life.

> Ignite the passion of praise
> To glorify
> To honor Your Name.

Dear Father,

Transform this humble life, the day by day routines. Fill my life with Your Presence hour by hour. Even, Lord, moment by moment. Stir my heart to praise You all through the days, never minding the silence, the seeming dullness, the emptiness. How could it seem so when You are here? There is always the Light of Your Presence, the Ladder to Your Throne, the Burning of Your Presence, and Your Word. You have said, "I will never leave you, not forsake you" (Hebrews 13:5). *Amen*

*   *   *   *   *

Breakthrough

Shiona was in the hospital. We were devastated and frustrated with the things doctors were telling us. They didn't give much hope for her coming out of the psychosis.

I was often at the library pouring through books trying to find someone somewhere who had lived through what our family was experiencing. All my searching uncovered nothing at the library or Christian bookstore, so I settled for whatever was on my bookshelf at home. Perhaps in all my reading I had missed something that would touch our situation. I decided to reread some old biographies and picked up *God's Man in China*, the story of Hudson Taylor. I was almost to the end of the book when this paragraph grabbed my attention:

"There is absolutely nothing to be done, but to bear the trial while using proper means, and wait on God. Our

171

house has been a hospital; it is now an asylum. All that this means only the Lord knows. The night and day strain are almost unbearable, but I know the Lord's ways are right, and I would not have them otherwise. So whatever time and care the case claims must be given and it must be pleasing to the Lord for us to be so occupied." *Thank You, Father.*

This was written on the occasion of the arrival of a group of young missionaries, one of which was in a state of acute mania. God sees and knows all about our human suffering. I'm sure Taylor didn't realize that these things would be passed down to us. But someday I will tell him that it was worth the reading of the preceding 300 pages to read that one short paragraph to which I could totally identify. It was the perfect word for me. I read it over and over.

"Bear the trial, use proper means, wait on God. It doesn't matter that our home is a psych ward. Night and day seems unbearable, but God knows, and it must be pleasing to Him to have us so occupied." Yes, if it pleases Him, since it is in His sovereignty to do otherwise. I believe He would if it were right for us and pleasing to Him. Certainly this was not medical information, but it was what I needed to hear. It was saying, "Go to the Source!"

Like when Jesus asked the man at the pool if he would like to be healed who said, "I have no man to help me," when Jesus was standing right in front of him (John 5:6-7)! Do we act like that sometimes? I know I have. It is best, like King David said, "Put the Lord ever before us" (Psalm 16:8). If He is before me, He is also between me and the situation. Think of it this way, you are approaching the check-out, the car wash, or the airport and you're hoping to be first in line. Suddenly someone steps right in front of you and you are sure you will miss the best opportunity; time is running out! It's hard to learn to keep Jesus in focus when confronting unexpected or undesired interruptions, isn't it? But then it is another growing experience. We forget real fast that Jesus is here for us. We can even talk to Him during the unwanted interruption; that could be the best news!

Four and a half months in the hospital was too long. But during this time at the wonderful suggestion of her doctor, Jay and I went puppy shopping. Oh, what a great idea. First, we asked Shiona for her ideas on having a puppy and what kind she favored.

"A Sheltie, of course," was her immediate response.

It didn't take long to find Lassie and plan her visit to the hospital to meet her new mistress! They made immediate friends. The supervising nurse even let Lassie come into Shiona's room (Shh- don't tell!). Now that was something to anticipate and something delightful waiting at home for hugs and tugs!

When Shiona came home, we had a job to do. We prayed and prayed for the Lord to show us and confirm to us that He was in this with us. Not just with us, her parents, but that He somehow lived through this with His child, for she is His child; that we could never doubt. This was when we were taking the same stand that Hudson Taylor did so many years ago. His words were a strong support to us. But how would this all work out? There was a lot of healing yet to be accomplished. We were anxious for the day that she would regain communication skills and the flattened affect would brighten.

"Bright eyes gladden the heart," says King Solomon in Proverbs 15:30. Believe me; I know bright eyes when I see them. Her usual bright eyes held no light. When she was well she had the biggest, brightest eyes and how they did gladden my heart. I missed the bright eyes; the light was gone. Neither did her face reflect any joy. Absent also was her spontaneity.

One day we were washing dishes, Shiona and I. She was drying; I was washing. My thoughts were searching again how to help her out of the cave she seemed to be living in. Several attempts at conversation didn't do anything and my heart sank. I could only ask Jesus to help her and bring her back to us. These were days when she was gathering multiple hugs from both of us in an effort to renew worth and confidence in her. With every display of affection and love, a pray for restored health; emotional, physical, and spiritual was directed upwards.

At that moment, hurt lodged in my heart as I looked into her face, so sad, so lost, so forlorn. Somehow I had to reach my daughter and to understand what was going on inside her. She seemed to be an empty shell beside me, going through the motions. Did you ever hold a seashell to your ear? You hear something, don't you? But from my daughter there was nothing, not even an echo. Where was Jesus in all this? Where was the Holy Spirit? Were they also trapped in this closed-off person who was so sad and empty? I wanted to know these things, to understand, but couldn't seem to find any answers. I was discouraged and baffled by this strange illness.

Time seemed to creep while we did this simple kitchen task. The atmosphere was heavy and still as we worked. But suddenly, quietly there started to come a song into the sad, blank moments. So softly it came. I looked at her. No change of expression; still distant and bleak, but the song came from far down inside of her. I could tell; it was her voice, now so tiny, weak, and high-pitched. My emotions were on tip-toe as I listened.

"Turn your eyes upon Jesus,
Look full in His wonderful face,
And the things of earth will grow strangely dim,

In the light of His glory and grace."
                        -Helen H. Lemmel

This was *Shiona* singing. It was something that had been
stored away in her heart and safely kept. The melody and the
words were both accurate and clear. There was no hesita-
tion. The song ended as a quiet thrill possessed me. At that
moment I turned my eyes to Jesus, consuming and devouring
this message, this compelling evidence: *Jesus is here!*

Letting the words sink deep into my spirit, with hands
dripping soap suds, I reached for her. I held her, hugged her
wrapping my arms tightly around her. I cried, I worshiped,
for I knew that Jesus by His Spirit was alive, living within
her! I knew now He suffered with her. She was not alone.

In times past I thought of the Lord helping us *in* our suffering and trials. Now I was seeing Him suffering *with* her
and us. I knew He would care, comfort, and bring everything
back to her and to us. She was not an empty shell and this
was more, so much more, than an echo. It was her voice, she
was right there with me, and the Spirit was singing with her.
This was truly a song in the night (Psalm 77:6), the long,
dark night of our agony. The answer for which I had been
crying out to God came from Shiona by His Spirit.

*Thank You, thank You, Dear Father, I am still praising
You for this!*

I will never forget the impact of that moment. How
poignant and penetrating was His answer to me. Like Jesus
said to Nicodemus, "The Spirit blows where it will, you
don't know where it comes from or where it goes" (John
3:8). At that moment I knew He was with her. She came to
Him while she was still a very young child and He would
never leave her. He was there all the time. How could I ever
doubt that He would live with her and with us through every
situation, tragedy, pain or grief? He would comfort and He

would heal and He would work through it all and never leave us or forsake us.

Now years later, Shiona is still disabled, but looking back I can agree with Hudson Taylor. Only the Lord knows the why, the duration, the care, and strain. Sometimes it may seem too much. But we know the Lord's ways are right, and we would not have them otherwise. It is surely pleasing to the Lord to have things as they are. Our will, our desires, and our preferences must die. Hudson Taylor helped me through this struggle, and helped me understand that in everything God's presence goes with us, without any doubt.

What we see now is beautiful. We can look at her and say with joy and enthusiasm, "Dear Shiona, your bright eyes surely gladden our hearts!" More than that we can stand back and say, "This is the Lord's doing, it is marvelous in our eyes!" *Thank You, Lord Jesus.*

* * * * *

She Smiles at the Future

Embracing the contradiction
She faces the daily affliction.
Just as the darkest night enhances the stars;
So His glory shines through too many scars.

The calm, the patient, the bending will,
Is His choice for the one standing so still.

Lo! The calm has escaped in the midst of turmoil.
But wait! Unexpected comes later the Godly spoil.

Confused and in the dark?
He knows!
And with another upward look

She wonders at the grace that flows
To quell returning fear.
She smiles!
Alive again! Surrounded now by living hope,
"She smiles at the future" (Proverbs 31:25).

Now may the God of hope fill you with all joy and peace in believing, that you may abound in hope by the power of the Holy Spirit. (Romans 15:13)

My soul, wait patiently for God alone, for my expectation is from Him. (Psalm 62:5)

The NAME of the
LORD is a strong
TOWER
the righteous runs into
it and is SAFE.
Prov. 18:10

Chapter Eleven

My Strong Tower

Teach Me, Lord

To bridge each moment-by-moment span
With acknowledgement of Your Presence.
To bridge each day-to-day endeavor
With songs in the night: Prayers to You.
To bridge each person-to-person encounter
With trust in Your preparation and wisdom.

Build bridges where You know there are
Rock-filled gullies,
Thorny, tangled ledges,
Raging, foaming waters.
Walk with me over these bridges,
Eyes fastened on You,
Not locked on the hazards,
or perils below.

Make my feet like hind's feet.
Walk with me hand in Hand
On the high places of Your choosing.
You are Love, You will show the Way.
I thank You, my Father

Teach me Thy way. O Lord, and lead me in a level path. (Psalm 27:11)

The Lord God is my strength, and He has made my feet like hind's feet, and makes me walk on my high places. (Habakkuk 3:19)

Do not be afraid, little flock. (Luke 12:32)

I will look after My sheep. (Ezekiel 34:1)

Teach me to do Thy will, for Thou art my God; let Thy good Spirit lead me on level ground. (Psalm 143:10)

Windows All Around

By the time you have read this far you have noticed that all the scriptures in the illustrations are placed in windows. I don't remember exactly how that came about, but one day while reading in Ezekiel chapter forty, I learned that in the new Temple there were to be many windows. "Windows all around" is repeated five times! Since I am a temple for His presence why would I not discover windows all around. If I have the Word of God in me, surely I have windows to look through.

I like to think that whatever happens, whatever our situation, we can find windows all around when we look to God in His Word for help and guidance. Perhaps that is why during the summer of 1994, I was searching for windows in His Word while Shiona was experiencing a slow and difficult recovery. As I sat with her, I was looking for windows of encouragement, strength, comfort, peace, joy, and hope. The window drawings with scripture became parables or pictures of many meditations throughout that summer, and also provided needed consolation for my mind and hands as I sat close by to be comfort and encouragement.

Windows on the Word, as I came to call them, have been undergirding and strengthening me many times for years. You probably have your own store-house of scriptures. They are also reminders of my Heavenly Father's constant I will never leave you nor forsake you promise (Hebrews 13:5). Some scriptures were rediscovered, having been underlined years ago, such as Ephesians 2:10, "For we are God's workmanship, created in Christ Jesus unto good works, which God prepared beforehand, that we should walk in them." It is so good to know that He is in all, around all, and above all! He even prepares works beforehand for us.

Another one is Philippians 2:13, *"For it is God Who is at work in you, both to will and to do of His good pleasure,"* brings forth the memory of a long, slow prayer meeting. In my impatience (I was still a teenager) I opened my Bible to Philippians and spent the rest of the prayer meeting time meditating on the revelation of God working in *me*. You could call it one of those precious stones shining forth from the gray stone boundaries around my life. It was saying to me, "Purpose, yes, let God do it and don't worry how it is to come about." Then some years later when my German boyfriend asked me to be his for always, Psalm 118:23-24 became our life verse, "This is the Lord's doing, it is marvelous in our eyes; this is the day the Lord has made, we will rejoice and be glad in it." What a life-long daily reminder *that* verse has been in the struggle to learn endurance, patience, daily strength, and the meaning of commitment. His Words have been windows of blessing in more ways than we could ever have anticipated in the early years.

It was while we lived in Oregon that we learned to sing, "Though the fig tree does not blossom and there be no fruit on the vine, the produce of the olive fail, and there be no herd in the stall, yet will I rejoice in the Lord, God the Lord is my strength" (Habakkuk 3:17-19 KJV). Only a short time later was that Word put to the test when the telephone call gave us the news no parent wants to hear, the accidental drowning of our son. In shock, we wanted to know all the answers to all our questions. That was not to be. But our Gracious Father met us with His Word. Yes, those Words were windows that we have dwelt on over and over. Our Father works in ways that we can never predict. His love is magnificent and powerful enough to pull us out of the deepest well. Only by His Holy Spirit can we respond with, "Yet will I rejoice in the Lord."

You read earlier about Robert's visit to us in New York at the end of summer. We were excited to show him all the surrounding areas that we knew would interest him. One of those places was a small Episcopal Church in Millbrook, New York. We didn't go inside that day, but it was only about two weeks later that we did go inside, only Robert was no longer with us. Our dear friends, Tom and Doris, chose to be our comfort, forfeiting their scheduled trip to Norway. Unknown to us, they exchanged their tickets for a flight to New York to precede our return after the Memorial service. The limousine that brought us from the airport pulled into our driveway. The porch lights were on, and Tom and Doris flung open our door to us! Tea and coffee cake were on the table. What warmth and love welcomed us home!

During their visit we drove to Millbrook and visited with them at that quaint little church which had fascinated Robert. When we walked into the church that day, I saw that the Bible on the pulpit was open, and said to Doris, "Let's go see if God left me a message!" I was always waiting for some Godly insight that would help set my heart at peace and soothe the constant ache. In the open Bible was a small note listing these Scriptures; Jonah 2, Psalm 29:10-11, and Luke 9:35-36.

In Jonah 2 we read, "While I was fainting away, I remembered the Lord; and my prayer came to Thee, into Thy holy temple. . . I will sacrifice to Thee with the voice of thanksgiving. That which I have vowed I will pay. Salvation is from the Lord." Yes, I stored these words in my heart.

Psalm 29:10-11 were verses I needed, "The voice of the Lord is upon the waters... The Lord sat as King at the flood. Yes, the Lord sits as King forever, the Lord will give strength to His people; the Lord will bless His people with peace."

In Luke 9:35-36 we read, "And a voice came out of the cloud, saying, 'This is My Son, My Chosen One; listen to Him!' And when the voice had spoken, Jesus was found alone."

Without a doubt and without explaining how, these scriptures were a strong comfort to me, answering or putting aside many questions. The overall message to me was *Look unto Him*. He was there at the river; as always He is the God who is there, present in every situation. I could take those verses and superimpose them on the tragedy at Clackamas River. I could visualize Jesus with Robert, because it says, "He sat as King at the flood of water," and then at the moment he left the river, his eyes were fixed and focused on his Lord and Savior. He saw Jesus alone in a new and better way. For me, where would I focus my eyes? Yes, for me too, it is to look nowhere but to Jesus, the One who loves me, the One who comforts me, the One who is welcoming Robert home.

Does our Father love us? Surely, surely He does! My words to Doris, "Maybe, God left me a message," came out of my mouth without forethought. I saw the open Bible and wanted desperately for Him to talk to me. He Did! Always, those moments in that quaint and lovely, small brick church, will be cherished and wondered at as long as I live. Those were sacred, precious moments, reading a message that my Father left for me. This was about a week after Robert went Home. These are Words that soothed the moments when I would sit in agonizing wonder about Robert's last moments of life here. Truly, our compassionate Father is here for the needy and the hurting. My thankfulness continues to rise to Him.

Words fail to convey it all, but I Thank You, Father.

*　*　*　*　*

My Strong Tower

Swiftly would one cast me down
Trample me down to ashen dust.
Now dare I quick take sword and shield
To battle with God's own Word - Be my Defender.

Cast far from me my sins, O Savior,
Create each day my heart renewed
Where written are Your Words of Promise:
To the end - To be My Savior.

Let my soul calm down before You
Away from heavy cares, or sadness
Of the day, that try to overtake each
Hour by passing hour - Be my Peace.

Let me rest in Your Son Jesus;
Help me find that confident trust
Jesus found in You His Father.
Faced with fearsome temptation - Be my Strong Tower.

Let Your Holy Spirit guide me daily
Teaching me from Your Holy Word.
Anoint my eyes to see Your ways,
To know the boundaries - Be my Guide.

Let me be drawn ever closer
To the spring of Living Water,
To the strength of sweet communion,
Lord of everlasting Life - Be my Well-spring.

*The Lord is my Rock, my Fortress, and my Deliverer,
even mine.* (2 Samuel 22:2)

*   *   *   *   *

Enablement

*There is a great heaviness when we carry,
Drag and clasp on to grievances,
Those myriad conflicts that we nourish and stroke
With our feeble strength.
Take away the breath and vitality of these ignoble thoughts,
Precious Jesus. Please bring them to naught.
Bind them like sheaves for the burning.*

*Take them, Jesus, pardon and
Rid me of the muck and grime;
So weighty within my heart just now.
It seems so easy to be offended.
But I would not be offended of You, my Jesus.
Rid me of this woeful temptation
To grovel and moan in self-pity.*

*To do for You what'er You ask
Is to be honored that You would trust me, even me.
To trust me so far and in the storm of it all
To bring gladness to Your heart, Dear Lord,
Is more honor than I deserve.
But so You have ordered Your Kingdom.*

*I would not cause reproach on Your Name
By showing a saddened face
In the duty to which You have called me.
Help me, Lord Jesus, to always look up,
To be burning and bright with Your joy.*

187

I need it, dearest Father — Your Joy!

*   *   *   *

Oops

Yesterday's prayer needed again today.
I traveled not far when weakened in strength.
The way was so steep, I stumbled and fell.
The path You kept hidden out of my view.
But the end came up clear,
May I say it again; "You are here!"
"I am here all along, always 'tis true."
Christ said long ago, "I'll never leave you. . .
No never, no never, no never leave you."

Child-like I come, I know not the way,
Take my hand, precious Savior,
Keep me close by Your side, showing the Way.
Your Name, it is written upon every step. Yet. . .
Seems lost in the ashes of worry and fret,
Though You remind so often - "I am ever so near."

The calm comes again, the quiet repose
With humble thanksgiving, with words. . .
Oh. . .Holy Spirit, help me compose.
Tune my heart, my dear Savior,
My love. . .I lift to You.

our God reigns

HOW LOVELY ON THE MOUNTAINS
ARE THE FEET OF HIM WHO BRINGS
GOOD NEWS, WHO ANNOUNCES PEACE
AND BRINGS GOOD NEWS OF HAPPI~
NESS, WHO ANNOUNCES SALVATION
AND SAYS TO ZION,"YOUR GOD REIGNS".
ISA 52:7

Chapter Twelve

Tokens of His Love

Two Trumpets - One Sound

Stay with me a little longer while we think about some things in a slightly different way.

What I am thinking about is again treasure in the trial. Now, however, think of "triumph in the tragedy." It is not strange to believers that Jesus suffered. Tragedy trailed Him since birth. But His Father had a great plan. It was necessary for God to use tragedy in order to display the triumphant victory. The trail followed Jesus all His life. First at birth, then as He served and ministered to all. Finally they thought they had Him in their grasp, those who continually accused Him. But Jesus endured, Jesus triumphed, and Jesus rose again. He put death to death! Jesus is the victor! Hallelujah! This is our King. Thus tragedy would never triumph again! Victim - NO. Victor - YES!

When you look at the drawing for this chapter title, you might think this a strange concept; two trumpets which are twins, actually Siamese trumpets joined at the bell. Tragedy and triumph together blend into one sound, a song of praise to the Sovereign God. When He sends or allows tragedy in our lives, there is always the promise of victory. Remember Job who said, "Shall we indeed accept good from God and not accept adversity?" (Job 2:10). Read in the last chapter of Job about his triumph! It is in the accepting, yielding, and believing in His sovereignty that leads us to victory. We would like to say, "Victory comes quickly." Why wait?

We may or may not see complete healing in this life. We may wait a long time to see what the Father has in store for our loved one who lives on with limitations or we yearn for the youth who lost his life. But it is certain that victory lies ahead for us. Maybe it takes a lifetime to see the evidence of victory. It can begin small and grow, as we have seen in our daughter's life. Or it can be waiting yonder as for our son. It is wonderful, yes, even marvelous but at this point not complete. God promises because His Son was willing to come live with us, to teach us, to heal us, and then to give His own life to redeem us, to cleanse us, and bring us into God's family.

Thinking of Jesus and how He shows us, as we sing, "Did e'er such love and sorrow meet or thorns compose so rich a crown." We meditate on that and thank Him for giving His life for us. Here is a Word from Philippians 1:29-30 that says, "For to you it has been granted for Christ's sake, not only to believe in Him, but also to suffer for His sake, experiencing the same conflict (contradiction) which you saw in me (Paul)." We meditate on that for a long while.

To Jesus on the cross they said, "Save Yourself, and come down from the cross!" (Mark 15:30). Can we expect any less? We still may hear people say, "Where is your Jesus, can't He do something?" Well, Jesus may do whatever He wants with His own. He may do something that many may not have eyes to see. So we are going to "run with endurance the race that is set before us, fixing our eyes on Jesus, the author and perfecter of faith, who for the joy set before Him endured the cross, despising the shame, and has sat down at the right hand on the throne of God" (Hebrews 12:1-2).

I am repeating myself when I again ask, "Can we not then endure and become more like Him in accepting what comes to us and thus give Him praise, glory and honor in our times of trial and testing?" In another place it says, "For you were called for the very purpose that you might inherit a blessing" (1 Peter 3:9). Do you like that one? I do!

So we can say trusting Jesus in the trial or tragedy brings triumph in the testing. There is a blast; you've heard the sound. It's a message of sorrow, grief or pain; a note you really don't want to read, a phone call or medical report you'd rather not hear; and it heralds tribulation or trial of some kind. But Christ asks us to trust, and in so doing we join our hearts to the Spirit to bring to life the trumpet call of triumph and victory. The Spirit helps us as we reaffirm our thanks unto God who causes us to triumph in our Lord Jesus Christ (1 Corinthians 15:57). Here's another look. Remember the words of Jesus, "Let your light so shine that men may see your good works and so glorify your Father in heaven" (Matthew 5:16). It may be easy to do this with happy things we love to do, but how about shining a light when it's a dark moment, a trying moment in our life?

How about letting our light shine when the candle is broken in that dark moment? My neighbor in New York was experiencing that dark moment after her son died in a motorcycle accident. I met her shortly after Robert died. She came over to my house many times to talk about her son. She would ask me again and again how I survived the death of my son. I would tell her it was by talking about Jesus and the gift of eternal life. She never seemed to get passed the sadness that her son was under the ground. He was gone and there was no display of pictures in their house, no visible memories. The many talks we had together never seemed to bring her relief, yet she came again and again. I can only pray that she finally gave up repeating her statement, "You can believe, but I can't." I didn't stop talking to her, but as long as we lived there, I never saw the bright light of life in her face.

Remember the man born blind in John 9:1-3? Jesus clarified this tragedy when He told those asking about who sinned, his man or his parents. Jesus amazed them when He said God would display His mighty works in this man's life. Who knows what message will be sent to unbelievers or down-cast believers when we willingly praise God in adversity? Neither do we know the arrival time of fruit from our testimony. But as those who believe, we can raise the triumphant sound of praise when, in our tragedy, we cling to the solace of His sovereignty, because our God reigns!

Heavenly Father, help us to bend our will to Yours, even when it is difficult and we don't know the reason; and keep crying, "Why?" Help us to accept and even thank You for what You are doing, so that You can show us the triumph in Christ's life and death and therefore the triumph for us in every situation. Only You can make a harmonious and triumphant sound out of human tragedy and divine sovereignty.

We praise Your Name, Holy Father, Amen.

*　　*　　*　　*　　*

Here Comes the Jesus Girl

Today Shiona and I went to Target to do a little shopping. When we were finished, it seemed a good moment for a quick refreshment.

"How about a small bag of popcorn?"

"Well, that would be all right for you, Shiona, but I think I will just have a drink while I watch you eat your popcorn. But, don't be surprised, I make eat a kernel or two!"

"Okay, then, if that's all you want," she laughed.

We found a table and chatted for a few minutes. When we got up to leave, she decided to go back to the counter and thank the young man who waited on her. I saw them laughing. Earlier he had seemed a bit sober. I thought, *She probably wanted to see a smile on his face before we left the store.* She caught up with me a few minutes later. I was already on the way to the car. Joy was written all over her face as she began to tell me about her encounter.

"I asked him if he knew the motorcycle handshake."

He said, "No."

"So I taught it to him and he liked it. Then I asked if I could sing him a song."

He said, "Sure, go ahead."

"What did you sing?" I asked.

"Oh, just something that came to my mind."

"You mean you never sang it before or heard it?"

"That's right. But he liked it a whole lot and asked if it was something I had heard, and was it recorded. I told him, no, that I just made it up."

He said, "Well, I sure liked it, and hope I will hear it again sometime."

She looked at me and said, "Someday you will hear it in heaven."

"Oh, was it about Jesus?" I asked.

"Yes, it was, and it made him smile. I think he will have a good day."

We left the Target store and drove on to our favorite Resale Shop, where she wanted to look for a dress for the holidays. It didn't take long and she found just what she wanted; denim combined with velveteen. With a few alterations it will be her new holiday dress.

As we were leaving, Shiona asked me, "Did you hear what that clerk said while we were looking around?"

"No, I didn't. What did she say?"

"Oh, no, there's that Jesus Girl again!"

195

We laughed together for a few minutes.

Then I said, "Well, Shiona, that is a good tag for you, don't you think? You are a real Jesus Girl. That is a good reputation. It's what you want to be."

I thought for a moment, "You know what? I might use it for a chapter title in my book! 'Here Comes the Jesus Girl'."

"Yeah, I like it," she said as I noticed again that look of joy on her face.

*   *   *   *   *

A long time ago in the Old Testament, there was a little girl who was captured by Syrians during a raid on the land of Israel. Now in captivity, she waited on a fine lady who was the wife of a Syrian general. He was also a leper. Being far from home, this young girl could have been crying in a corner; instead, she bravely went to her mistress with a message. It was a message of good news. She told her mistress that if the general would go to the prophet in Israel, he could be healed. But he was a stubborn, proud man, and he put up a struggle. Finally though, after a lot of coaxing, he followed the prophet's instructions and dipped seven times in the Jordan River. Amazed, he came up clean, and went home with skin like a little child. Read the story in 2 Kings 5.

In the New Testament we read about another little girl. She was very sick and died before Jesus got to her house. Though the family friends laughed at Jesus, He took her hand, spoke to her and her spirit returned. She got up and her mother brought her food to eat. Luke 8:41-42; 49-56 is where you will find the story of Jairus' twelve-year-old daughter. Don't you think she had a special story in her heart? What a wonderful way to meet Jesus!

I think of these two girls as Jesus Girls. Jesus said to go into all the world with the Good News. Each of us has a portion of that world around us. Our age doesn't matter, just knowing Jesus should give us the desire to share the Good News. You don't have to be super smart or especially clever. We can just remind the world, wherever we go, that there is Someone who is bigger than us. When we are doing so, we are glorifying our Father and His Son, Jesus Christ.

Jesus said, "These things I have spoken to you, that My joy may be in you, and that your joy may be made full." (John 15:11)

Blessing Him in All Places

In the kitchen
In the garden
In the laundry
Or the sickroom
Bless the Lord.

In the office
In the schoolroom
In the prison
Or the pew
Bless the Lord.

In the family
In the city
In the church
Or in the country
Bless the Lord

In the nearness
In the distance
In the darkness
Or the gloom
Bless the Lord.

In my thoughts
In my feelings
In my sadness
Or despair
Bless the Lord.

In the sunlight
In the shadow
In every turning
Hear my prayer
of blessing, Lord.

Bless the Lord, O my soul, and all that is within me bless His Holy Name. (Psalm 103:1)

Every day I will bless Thee, blessed be the name of the Lord from this time forth and forever. (Psalm 145:2)

From the rising of the sun to its setting, the name of the Lord is to be praised. (Psalm 113:2-3)

* * * * *

Take Hold of My Hand

In a recent reading of one of the CIM (China Inland Mission) stories, I paid attention to a specific insight that Hudson Taylor wrote regarding people contact. I had read this particular book several times, but it took my own personal experience of observing similar struggles in a different context to really absorb the intent. The incident comes right out of Taylor's experience in a Chinese village. It is a touching story.

"A poor woman in a certain village when she heard of Mrs. Riley's death (a CIM missionary) and said; 'What a loss to us! She used to take hold of my hand, and comfort me so. . .'" He went on to say; "There is a mighty power in contact. . . . They are not clean, and sometimes we are tempted to draw our skirts together; but I believe there is no blessing when that is the case. . ." (speaking, of course, of poor, neglected Chinese laborers in his place of ministry). "There is much power in drawing near to this people, and there is a wonderful power in touching people. If you put your hand on the shoulder of one there is power in it. . . there is something in contact; it is a real power we may use for God." From memories, he recalls, "Those were days of the touch of the hand, the loving concern in the eyes, the simple testimony of the voice. They would not be forgotten later on when the government forbade it."

The time did come when the Communist government forbade the smallest human connection. That is exactly what happened for Wilda Mathews, a CIM missionary with her husband Arthur in 1951, when she learned that a few loving words, smiles, and perhaps a touch were to be the only direct ministry she was to have among the Chinese women. Nevertheless, it was enough for them to comprehend she was there to love them. Later, when forbidden that miniscule association, the Chinese women did not forget the touch of care from the white woman living among them.

I think that our Father would not want us to minimize the blessing we can pass on to those with limitations. We could misunderstand by thinking they don't know or cannot interpret or grasp wordless ministrations that say, "I care." The smallest overture is never overlooked by one longing for acknowledgement or by our Heavenly Father. Again comes to mind that small saying from long ago, "Little is much when God is in it!"

I have seen the gratitude and stimulation brought about by the smallest inclination toward one with immense limitations. I have seen the gratefulness on the face and in the eyes of a parent who, within him/herself longs for another to come alongside and in a simple loving way, acknowledge his/her child of special needs. Our Father does not waste or overlook the smallest blessing given in His Son's name. Someone has said, "Each small kindness, like a seed, grows tall in memory."

She was dressed in pink, the young teenager sitting with her parents in the taco restaurant. Shiona saw her immediately and went to greet her, while Jay ordered our lunch. She was a stranger to Shiona, but only for moments while being complimented on how pretty she looked in pink.

Jay brought our food to the table and we began eating, when Shiona asked me, "Do you still have that cute pink pencil with the pink animal shaped eraser I gave you?"

"Sure, it's right here in my purse. Do you want it?"

"Oh, please, yes I do," and as I gave it to her, she took a small pink notepad out of her purse. "Excuse me a minute, I'll be right back."

Off she went to the cute gal in pink. Well, I could see without staring how happy she made her friend. But most of all, her parents' eyes spoke volumes of gratefulness that a "stranger" had given special love to their daughter with special needs.

Thank You, Lord Jesus, for Your love.

A small kindness can also fill our hearts with great expectation. Shiona does not see Addie anymore; we have moved too many times to faraway places. It was while we were living in Oregon that these two girls met in third grade. Addie was different. Addie didn't understand a lot of things, but that didn't matter to Shiona. This was an opportunity.

She knew she could help Addie learn about some of the playground equipment during recess. Besides that, they spent a lot of time just hang'n out.

Then Addie started going to Sunday School with Shiona. She started memorizing verses. We could hear them reciting in the back seat of the car going to and from church. She was learning about Jesus, and never wanted to miss a Sunday. Then one day out on the playground, Addie knelt down with Shiona to ask the Lord Jesus into her heart. It must have been an unusual sight on the playground! However, Shiona and Addie didn't care about that or even notice it. They were doing important business. Jesus' love was there!

It wasn't long after when we moved, again. But Addie and her mother had a thank-you gift for Shiona so she would always remember the special friendship they enjoyed. This friendship will someday be reunited on that Day when Jesus will reveal all the Great Expectations! Many Great Expectations will be gleaned from these small attentions given without any forethought or planning, just obeying the quiet inspiration.

Greater Love

Testing came like the blast of winter,
That day when we learned of the hurt.
Afraid of an oppressive burden,
We feared of both flood or flame.

Our foot He allows not to slip on the way
To the abundant place He prepares;
To peace that is greater than burden,
And trust without earthly compare.

As Guide He is always before us,
Lending His hand to hope.

201

His truth and justice are worthy of trust;
He'll heed always the earnest prayer.

There's far more treasure than can be seen
In the vessel that's bruised or scarred.
Spend what will never come to an end:
God's love - it's greater than any who's marred.

To bring kindness to the weak and lonely,
Christ shows how His work is done:
Amid the crowds He graciously mingles and looks,
For the needy, lame and the oh, so young.

Midst multitudes maybe there's one
Who needs just a kindly touch -
A warm, loving hand on his flesh just once -
But Christ reaches his heart instead.

Now, when I place my hand on just one,
One who has longed for a touch or embrace;
My heart fills up with a sacred joy,
When I think of my God in the flesh.

It was the will of the Lord that His servant grow like a
plant taking root in dry ground, He had no dignity or
beauty to show. . .We despised Him and rejected Him
sore; He endured pain and suffering He did not deserve;
and none would even look at Him there. We ignored Him
as if He were nothing. (Isaiah 53:2-3)

He endured it to open the Door!
Thus He teaches us now to remember
The needy, the young, and the lame,
Lest we, not wanting to see the hurt,
Ignore our dear Savior the same.

* * * * *

Jesus in the Midst

Lord Jesus, midst the disarray
Kindly extend Thy peace.
Thou art my soul's supreme support;
Be ever near.

Tenderize my heart, dear Lord,
However painful this may be;
And sow Thy seed in ready soil
To grow and multiply.

Cause me to hear Your Word,
Let me know Thy touch,
Bring forth Thy love, Thy joy,
In my life to reign, my King.

Sanctify my thoughts,
My words, my doings,
For Thine own good pleasure;
Thou only to glorify.

* * * * *

Tokens of His Love

The dictionary says a token is anything indicative of another thing; a sign, tangible proof or evidence; a signal or pledge. It is evidence of something; a souvenir or keepsake. We are all familiar with the giving of the wedding ring with the words, "In token and pledge." It is the characteristic symbol of something significant.

I find that God is abundant in offering tokens of the love, care, and protection He has toward His people. The first we read of tokens is in Genesis after the flood. God said, "This is the token of the covenant which I make between Me and you and every living creature. I set my bow in the cloud, and it shall be for a token" (Genesis 9:12-17 KJV). Don't you love to stand outside with your little ones after a storm and explain what God has promised as you look at the rainbow? Even after thousands of years, the rainbow means nothing less than what God spoke to Noah after the flood. As I read His Word which is also itself a bountiful token of His love, He prompted me to accept many tokens of protection, care, and promises of a glorious future with Him. King David asked, "Show me a token for good" (Psalm 86:17 KJV). He wanted those who hated him to know God's power, comfort, help, and protection.

In praying for Shiona, I have seen what seems obvious to me how our Father provides her with many tokens of love and affirmation coming from Him in His own distinct way. Here are some observations of His love-tokens.

In the midst of doctor visits, tests, and consultations we took time out for exercise. Walking in the mall, eating lunch out occasionally, and visiting stores which gave us opportunities for a bit of socializing. Shiona is good at making brief conversation with someone she has never before met. A little chat here and there can be quite delectable to a person whose social life has hovered around medical professionals. You feel like saying, "Open the window, life is getting a little stuffy."

To the surprise of us all, our Heavenly Father began providing her with some minutes-long encouragements and little astonishments along the way. These special encounters could be called tokens of His love and reminders of promises to be fulfilled.

At the Talbot's store (oh, how she loves to shop!), she spoke Jesus' name to the sales clerk who responded immediately with, "I believe in Him, too."

Then began a bright, delightful conversation between these two, and reminders of a vast future to share. A choice few moments for sure, and I wasn't surprised when Shiona slipped off the bracelet she had made for herself and handed it to her new friend.

Then one day, almost colliding with a third person while we were entering the library, Shiona, in her uninhibited way, said, "Goodness, you are wearing my favorite color today!"

"I am?" questioned the lady as she looked down at her clothing, "Is it purple?"

"Yes, it is and do you know why it's my favorite color?"

"No, I don't, please tell me."

"Because Jesus wore purple and He died to save us from our sins!"

"Amen," said the new friend as she lifted her hand for a "high-five" and gave her own testimony of her faith in Jesus.

So it goes, day after day, encounter after encounter; tokens of love from our Father above as Shiona spreads cheer and encouragement wherever she goes, greeting Kingdom citizens with reminders of future meetings. In an amazing way, she is passing around God's love with a smile, bright eyes, a touch, a handshake, a high-five or a hug. Actually these love tokens in many cases are going in two directions. At times any of us can be a signpost or road mark (Jeremiah 31:23) for a searching or hungry soul without being aware.

Perhaps a smile, a hug, a verbal exchange will lift Jesus higher, which goes with His promise: "If I be lifted up, I will draw all men unto Me" (John 12:32). Jesus tells us we are lights in our generation. The world is in darkness without His light. What a high privilege to be Light bearers. One day Shiona was asked how it felt when she happened to be speaking to a non-believer.

She answered, "I flutter a bit inside, that's all." Sounds so easy!

Christmas was coming soon, we were in Penney's and Shiona, ever on the look-out for an opportunity, went to an older lady to comment on her lovely hairdo.

Much to her astonishment came the reply, "How nice of you. I didn't know how my hair looked today. I did the best I could. You see, I have a bad problem with my eyesight right now and I was hoping I looked okay today. I have so many things to get done. You have just made my day. I can go on now knowing I am looking just fine. Thank you, so much."

It may not sound like a Gospel invitation, but spreading an encouragement and a happy word can do more than we dare to think.

Lord, help me be a signpost. It may be to one who knows not the way, or for a time has lost the way, is perhaps confused, but You know. So, Lord, help me be a road mark, a reminder of Your love.

I asked Shiona one day what influenced her to boldly speak to people about Jesus. She recalled that when she was about eleven or twelve years old she started reading about Corrie ten Boom. She was awed by Corrie's survival in Nazi concentration camps, and her avowed promise to her sister Betsy to take the Good News wherever God would lead her. She said it made a very strong impression on her and that from then on she had a desire to be like Corrie.

While the physical and mental struggles have been life-long since age seven; to tell as many as possible about Jesus, and to pray for them has been a life-long desire. Her testimonies are short, but I always like to recall the scripture, "His name is an ointment poured forth" (Song of Solomon 1:3KJV) Just saying His Name has power in it. It is soothing, it is refreshing, and can help someone turn a difficult corner. We don't know, but God knows and nothing, even so slight as a smile, is unnoticed by Him. What a privilege to spread the fragrant aroma of the Son of God!

Our family was privileged to hear and see Corrie when she gave one of her final appearances in Portland. She came on stage driving a golf cart; that was touching in itself, and an indication she was not about to slow down. Corrie spoke in a challenging way about God's grace in times of difficulty, and the rewards when she had an opportunity to tell someone about Jesus. The ongoing impact is noticeable, as Shiona treasures her books, and Corrie's picture is one of her special possessions.

It was a day that started out with the familiar words of Charlotte Elliot's hymn in my thoughts, "fightings within and fears without, O Lamb of God, I come, I come." This stopped me short and made me wonder, "What is ahead this day?" It was a tense morning. The atmosphere was tight, and Shiona seemed overwhelmed and not so able to comprehend, as Jay and I lent ourselves to the need. The words of the hymn seemed to be an indication of what this morning was to be. However. . .the day ended with Praise and Victory. We were at K-mart when Shiona recognized and reached out to a young man with Down syndrome and his mother.

Right away she said to him, "I think I remember you from a class we were in together. I hope you are doing well."

She touched him on the shoulder as they chatted together. His mother's face showed the obvious pleasure that someone recognized her son, and not only that but in so doing was affirming him as a fellow human being of worth. It was a grand token for him, as he was also pleased and expressed himself to Shiona.

Tokens, surprise encounters, words fitly spoken, simple words, but carrying the message that says, "Hey, you are okay, and I remember you!" I am still in awe as I watch these little happenings. Each one is a stake in the path of someone that stands out as a road mark, a guidepost of approval and affirmation in someone's life. It is a secret ministry, a ministry of Jesus' love as He gives her the impulse to make a connection.

This is the Lord's doing, it is marvelous in our eyes. (Psalm 118:23)

The names are many, and we can't recall them all, but recently it was Janet, a clerk at Wal-mart. Discovering they share not only their name (Shiona is Gaelic for Janet, which means, gracious gift of God), but also found they share faith and love for Jesus. A shopping trip to Wal-Mart always includes a warm exchange, another token of love.

Then there is Joyce with the tattoo on her arm, who we met at Gordman's. The tattoo seemed to urge an introduction: "Your name is Joyce!" That was easy, but quickly she told how she regretted it and wished she could cover it up with a picture of Jesus. She liked the suggestion that Joyce could become Rejoyce. That led again to the shared joy of shared faith, the Father's surprise for Shiona that day.

We didn't say good-by until Joyce told us the story of her three grandchildren, two of whom have a rare condition called Neiman Pic disease type C. (You can join your prayers with ours and others for Brisan and Parker.) They will not live a long life, but we believe with their grandmother and parents that they will be everything God wants them to be both here and in heaven. Joyce has become a supporting and comforting friend over the past several years. Every time we see her, she has a special word for Jesus and joy is her emblem!

A few days ago at one of Shiona's favorite stores, she asked another customer, "Could I ask you a question? If you don't want to answer it's okay. Are you Italian?"

"Well, I am," she answered, "And my name is Maria. God bless you."

"God bless you, too," was just the beginning of recognizing another follower of Jesus along with the invitation to visit her church.

"I will be there, Shiona, when you come."

Over and over again, God is showing Shiona what she has long desired; love, approval, and affirmation which translates to, "I'm okay, I belong here. Even with my disabilities and limitations, Jesus is showing me He loves me."

My message is, "Don't be afraid to spend what will never be exhausted, God's love."

If we reach out, God will reach right back with more than we can carry. When we share a token of God's love with another, God will surely give us a token of His love in return. He is never our debtor. His love endures forever. He is love, and His love is boundless. 1 Peter 4:8 tells us, "Perfect love casts out fear." It is not always easy to start talking to a stranger. But as I see Shiona doing what God asks her to do, I realize it is His love that imparts the strength to hug a stranger. As we receive love and learn to spread love we become stronger because God's love is strengthening power, and with His love, we are pushing back the enemy. I see this happening in my own daughter's life. "Out of the mouths of babes Thou hast established strength. . .to make the enemy and revengeful cease" (Psalm 8:2). Aren't we all babes in His kingdom?

See how great a love the Father has bestowed upon us, that we should be called children of God. (1 John 3:1)

How lovely on the mountains are the feet of him who brings good news, who announces salvation, and says to Zion, "Your God reigns!" (Isaiah 52:7)

Chapter Thirteen

A Still Small Voice

Tender Mercies for the Lambs

Little tears?
Jesus! - Close enough to wipe those little tears.

A little sigh?
Jesus! - Close enough to hear the faintest sigh.

A little hurt?
Jesus! - Close enough to feel the smallest hurt.

A little frown?
Jesus! - Close enough to soothe the troubled brow.

A little prayer?
Jesus! - Close enough to answer the feeblest prayer.

A little faith?
Jesus! - Close enough to strengthen even fragile faith

A little one?
Jesus! - Close enough to carry the frailest one.

Who despises the day of small things? (Zechariah 4:20)

It is not the will of your Father in heaven that one of these little ones be lost. (Matthew 18:16)

The Lord is great. . .in loving-kindness. The Lord is near to all who call upon Him. (Psalm 145:8, 18)

He is looking through the windows. He is peering through the lattice. (Song of Solomon 2:9)

He is touched with the feelings of our infirmities. (Hebrews 4:1)

The Lord is at hand. (Philippians 4:5)

*   *   *   *   *

A Mother's Prayer

Do Thou for her, dear Lord,
For her, a word, a call, a voice,
A note that comes with
Love entwined to show
Thy love, Thy care;
Lift, Lord, her discouraged heart.

Do Thou for her, dear Lord,
One for whom Thou has died;
To lift the lowered eyes, dear Lord,
And fill with rays of light -
Thy light, Thy care;
Calm, Lord, her anxious heart.

Do thou for her, dear Lord,
A touch, a hand, an embrace
With Thy tenderness; her heart
Secure, in the family of
Thy love, Thy care;
Heal, Lord, her wounded heart.

*   *   *   *   *

Doing It Differently

Praise be to the God and Father of our Lord Jesus Christ,
the Father of compassion and the God of all comfort,
who comforts us in all our troubles, so that we can com-
fort those in any trouble with the comfort we ourselves
have received from God. For just as the sufferings of
Christ flow over into our lives, so also through Christ
our comfort overflows. If we are distressed, it is for your
comfort and salvation; if we are comforted, it is for your
comfort, which produces in you patient endurance of the
same sufferings we suffer. And our hope for you is firm,
because we know that just as you share in our suffer-
ings, so also you share in our comfort. (2 Corinthians
1:3-7 NIV).

W hat did Jesus see when He looked at the multitudes?
He saw them distressed and downcast. He saw those
who were blind, lonely, crippled and lame, and felt compassion. He saw them as sheep without a shepherd (Matthew
9:36). He never passed by a needy sheep. He knew their
pain. By contrast, we don't want to see or feel the pain, the
need, or the distress. Naturally, we are looking for those
with whom we can make conversation and shake hands (uh
oh! maybe they can't extend a hand!), especially when it
is someone we haven't met before. But that person is there

and he stands or sits maybe in a wheelchair. He is someone who we observe is battling with a disability. We try to shield ourselves from it. It is often unpleasant, persistent and is limiting. It is an interruption in our plans. What shall we do? Mask it (if it is our own), hide it (if it is someone dear to us) or look away because we don' t know them anyway. Could we learn from Jesus?

Perhaps we have no awareness of one in the body who is struggling. We believe all is okay because we go to all lengths to cover and hide it. Yes, we do! We don't like to be exposed. But Jesus says we *can* learn. It's a hard thing to admit if we don't care, but more than likely we do care, we just don't know what to say or do. Maybe we are members of a desensitized society (could be true), that does not see or feel the pain that is happening in the community. The more we are desensitized, the more we can overlook the victims of disability, abuse or neglect. If this washes over into the Body of Christ because of the negative direction of our culture, how is the Body (*it is* His Body) to function in unity, in healing, in helping, in strengthening, and encouraging one another?

Healing is a normal activity in the human body, just as God intends for that to be a normal function in His Body. The hurting ones in the Body of Christ cry out for healing and repair just as the hurting member in our physical body cries for the forces that will aid healing. In both cases we know that we *know* the healing is inherent in the body! The member in pain seems to know this best in the immediate need and in the observed need. I believe we all know it.

We were shopping one day shortly before Christmas. The lines were a bit long and there was a wheelchair in the line with the rest of us.

"Oh, no, this is going to take longer than usual," you could hear the remarks, because the young man needed extra help. People looked at one another, maybe hoping for some kind of solution to hurry things up in this hurry-up-I'm-busy-world.

However, the only thing that happened had the potential to make transactions longer. One of the shoppers turned to the young man in the wheelchair and started talking to him. It quickly became obvious to all those around that he was not only crippled but also a deaf-mute.

You could almost hear the thoughts, "How could that lady prolong things with trying to 'talk' to a deaf-mute?"

But someone who cared was with him to push the wheelchair (his hands couldn't do it). She began interpreting with her hands, and what a conversation the young lady had with the gentleman in the wheelchair! Goodness, after the conversation she even patted his shoulder and wished him, "Merry Christmas and Jesus bless you," with a brief hug. Everyone could see how thrilled he was by the enormous smile that covered his face!

"Really, did you ever, it didn't take so long after all, and wasn't he blessed," eyes followed as we walked on our way.

Sometimes our reaching out to a needy family is planned and sometimes it goes differently than planned. That's what happened when we stopped at a friend's house to make a delivery on a wintry day. After a happy visit, we reached for our warm winter coats. No sooner had Shiona put her coat on, than she took it off, handing it to Doretha.

"This is for you, Jesus wants you to have it."

"O honey, goodness, how did you know I needed a coat?" Doretha exclaimed.

"Jesus let me know," was the quiet response and we said our good-bye with lots of hugs.

Later in our warm car, Shiona reflected on the fact that Jesus would supply the coat she also needed. But the joy of spontaneously rushing to the need of another, thinking of her friend walking to the children's school, doctor, grocery store, hospital, and many times to the bus stop for a long-awaited bus, three children in tow, eclipsed her own need. After all, we were snuggly warm, and we could buy another coat.

Now I was to learn something about my daughter. She had accomplished the secret desire to give in an adventurous way. The background is the story of David Wilkerson going barefoot to his car after removing his shoes and handing them to a needy teenager on the streets of New York city.

"Mom," she told me, "I remember reading about that, and I always wanted to know how that would feel to just hand somebody something they needed and I would go without."

Surprising is the fact that she continues this secret passion. Jesus likes to astonish His children in the adventure of giving and receiving. It's all part of the learning, and learning to do it differently when He says, "Obey."

Even Jesus learned obedience from the things which He suffered (Hebrews 5:8). Does it not follow that it is also how we learn, particularly as we hear Him saying, "I desire compassion" (Matthew 9:13). We learn by embracing, not resisting! The embracing part takes learning and practice and lots of watching and listening. If this is too much for us, then perhaps Jesus' suffering on the cross is also too much for us. We really have a patchwork religion with a little of Him and a little more of the way the world looks at life.

Have you ever thought of yourself as a *"least-of"* (Matthew 25:40)? Have you ever received a cup of cold water? Maybe a thirst-quenching drink of the water I shall give (John 4:14). In coming to Christ, surely we have all realized ourselves as least-of. Yet we bear the image of God, giving evidence of being indwelt even in a malfunctioning body. Does God absent Himself because of the mental dysfunction or bodily limitations? No. I cannot think so, since He freely offers us a Living Hope, and a future Life that is beyond description.

So then, how important must be the tender mercies to our Lord Jesus. . .even that cup of cold water. The One who gave back her son to the unnamed widow, does He not care for the least ofs? Let's ask ourselves, do we know a "least-of" who needs a touch of tender mercy? Then let Jesus visit one of them through you. Indeed they are all around us, like the young man in the wheelchair; we may never know his name, but Jesus knows and He also knows who showed tender mercy. Surely we can identify because each of us has been and still is a least of. He brought us to Himself "just because." Not because there was merit in us. If we have received the Lord's tender mercy, we know what the tender mercies are. So let's not be afraid to make a delivery in His Name.

A question to ask ourselves: Are we close enough to see the need of a tender mercy? Most likely there is that need very close to each of us, so let's be bold enough and draw close enough in the strength and will of our Tender Shepherd. Let's move close enough to be touched by the feeling of another's weakness, and administer a touch of tender mercy. Let's stay long enough to listen, if necessary. How else can we know how heavy the heart is, the heart of the caretaker or the heart of the one being cared for.

We can also "pray as though we were in prison with them, and those who are ill-treated," says Paul in Hebrews 13:3. That is being close enough to *feel* the loss, the pain, the disappointment and not just saying, "Oh, you'll get over it, this happens to everyone. Oh, don't cry." It may be an interruption, to be sure, but doing it differently takes *real* compassion; which means, feeling the same feeling with that person's grief, hurt or struggle. It cannot be passed off with quick phrases, it must come from within.

Surely we have learned in the bringing of children into our lives the need for tender care, compassion, and under-standing. In our own crying out in suffering for we will all suffer, it is promised that the Father of tender mercies and God of all comfort has been holding us, caring for and loving us in and through all sorts of conflict, weakness, loneliness, and grief. This is not for our hoarding because when we see and are touched by another's desperate situation, Jesus' tenderness flows through us, even while sitting still and holding a hand. Even our own soul is comforted when we pour through His Word, praying those very Words as our own prayer.

The very life of the wounded cries for help. Job 24:12

Dear Father, Your tender mercies are always available. Even as You are close enough, teach us to draw closer to You and to others. Thank You, dearest Father, for teaching us about Your tender mercies. The Word is true: You are the barrier against any fear, any hurt, any pain. You hold us in Your Hand! Father, You and Your Son are there for the faintest, the frailest, the smallest. You are there, and we trust You; for You keep us, You hold us, You love us. Thank You, dearest Father. In Your Word You said, "If you have done it unto one of the least of these, you have done it unto Me." Help us to follow closely. In Jesus Name, Amen.

* * * * *

Ministry of Love

As He prayed to the Father and His friends stayed nearby,

Not calm but fitful sleep captured them into defeat.

The sweat of blood was heavy upon a gentle brow,

As He searched the dark blue sky for an answer to the why.

Finally His sleeping friends slowly came awake,

When Jesus then sought for a word with which He spake.

The contrast of joy and care, instead it was warning

Mingled with despair:

"Peter, oh Peter, please listen, little one, I love you as my
only fleshly son.

At three o'clock tomorrow you shall find yourself in sorrow.

You will deny my precious Name with a bitter cursing stain.

Since your life means more to you than relationships of pain."

As I read this lonely passage, it came to me - a low and
distant plea,

To watch my step more closely for what the cost had
meant to Thee.

I want to give myself more fully in Your ministry of love,

To have a gift of mercy during the days which seem so thirsty.

For at least a bitter cup in which a friend and I shall sup –

To be a useful vessel, even though my soul will wrestle.

I give my heart, mind and body unto Thee

For the rest of a blessed and glorious eternity.

Shiona Ann Muthmann

A Comment on Shiona's Poem

This poem of Shiona's written when she was still in
middle teen years, could have easily been laid aside. I am

thankful it was not ignored, but put carefully away. The years passed as her life unfolded into a journey we could never have anticipated. What we as her parents have come to see is that God undeniably took her prayer, recorded as part of this poem, seriously. As you continue to read, I hope you can also see that God's hands have enfolded her life in a divine way for the fulfillment of His purpose in her. The limitations of her pathway have provoked in her the necessity for a deep relationship with her Savior. She often struggles with a hurt feeling (she is tender-hearted) or disappointment. Still these struggles are shortly given over to songs of praise. Is she one of the babes spoken of in Psalm 8, one who has been ordained to praise? God knows. It seems her life He has captured for Himself, regardless of limitations, perhaps because of them. She has often said to me, "It is good that God clipped my wings, who knows where I would be today if He hadn't!" She is not sad in saying that. Sure, there are longings, and Jesus in His way takes care of those also. It was in His plan to gift her with words and music that exalt Him. They are short and quick, she can seldom recapture them, so she says, "You will hear it someday again - in Heaven!" She moves through life as a melody. Often when I have a weary time or a negative attitude, she will do her best to sing me out of it. She sings of Jesus and to Him, talks of Him and to Him, listens to Him and leans on Him. Jesus is her life.

Jesus said, *"Because I live, you shall live also."* (John 14:19)

We say it again, thank You, gracious Father.

* * * * *

Come Unto Me

In the quiet of the morning
Through the rush and rattle of the day;

Clutching tightly unto Jesus
Is the only trusted way.

He in mercy stands ready, waiting,
With affirming words at early light.
Refreshed by sleep or peacefully resting,
Find in Jesus true delight.

By Him, for Him, with Him, in Him;
'Tis the life He planned for me.
Teach me in my daily struggles
Better how to lean on Thee.

Teach me to pray, teach me to think;
Give me words to worship intent.
To simply rest in Your blest Presence
Is communion calm, renewed, content.

*   *   *   *   *

Lord, I Need Thee

Lord, I need Thee,
How I need Thee —
Need Thy breast to lean upon.

Lord, I need Thee,
How I need Thee —
Need the strength of Thy strong arms.

Lord, I need Thee.
How I need Thee —
Need fresh comfort at Thy side.

223

Lord, I need Thee,
How I need Thee —
Need to hear Thy loving Words.

Do not fear, for I am with you; do not look anxiously about you, for I am your God. I will strengthen you, surely I will help you, surely I will uphold you with My righteous right hand. (Isaiah 41:10)

*   *   *   *   *

He Answers Every Call

Why do I waver when You are near?
Do not fear, draw near, just draw near.

Why do I hesitate when You have spoken?
Follow on, follow on and listen.

Why do I thirst when You will fill?
Drink deeply, deeply from the Well

Why so anxious when You have overcome?
Lean hard, lean hard on Me.

Why regard pettiness when You are the Almighty?
Humbly bow, humbly bow in worship.

Why discouraged when You are the God of Hope?
Courage, My child, take courage.

Why weary when You are the God of strength?
Come rest, come rest and abide.

224

Why sad when the God who sustains is at hand?
Joy, take joy and rejoice.

*   *   *   *   *

A Cup of Cold Water

Putting the shopping bags in the car, I handed Shiona the stickers she just bought, thinking she would like to look them over on the drive home. On such a hot day, I was already in the car getting it air conditioned while she returned the shopping cart to its place. As we backed out of our space I slowed for someone coming in our direction on her way into the store. She waved eagerly and smiled brightly at Shiona who returned the greeting.

"Is that someone you know?" I asked.

"No, she was just getting out of her car when I returned the shopping cart."

"Did you get to have a little chat?"

"Yes, we did. She seemed very nice."

That was the end of the conversation and we went on to other errands. Later, at home, I wondered aloud about the stickers she was so eager to buy.

"Oh, the stickers, I gave them to that lady. I just felt they were for her!"

No more questions, I just knew that once again Jesus asked her to give a "cup of cold water" on a very wearing and warm day.

A few days later I was reading in a devotional book on the topic of Matthew 19:42, "If anyone gives even a cup of cold water. . . he will certainly not lose his reward." At the end of the few paragraphs was a quote from Henry Wadsworth Longfellow, "Give what you have, for you never know - to someone else it may be better than you can even dare to think." Inside I am saying, *"Thank you, Lord Jesus,*

225

You have given us a daughter whom You have gifted with such a giving heart!"

Then one day at the Chinese lunch buffet, Shiona excused herself from the table. Thinking to myself, "Am I going to witness another cup of cold water? Yes, of course, it is her life, and oh, how much I can learn about the giving spirit." Later she told me that she sang to one of the older Chinese servers. Shiona probably observed her working hard, going back and forth to serve her customers, and thought, "She needs a lift to her spirits right now." *May the words linger and cause her more thirst for You, Lord Jesus!*

I cannot help wondering at the Words of Jesus, "even a cup of cold water." Think of Him sitting at the well asking a woman for a drink and how she tried to explain to Him that He shouldn't be asking her for water because He was a Jew. That gave Jesus His opportunity to invite her to the water He could give her. She answered, "You have nothing to draw with." We know the Well that never runs dry was her reward that day. Not only for her, but for the whole town! (John 4).

Jesus never scolds for not having something to draw with because He knows we each are an empty vessel waiting to be filled. So when He shows us someone, we can always respond with whatever we have to give. The gift itself, even if it is only a spontaneous song that honors Him, a simple bracelet, a card of stickers or a word of encouragement, the love that causes it to be passed on can multiply in the hungry heart. When the recipient who wasn't even asking for anything says in her/himself, "I didn't ask for a card of stickers, a song, a tube of lotion, or a handshake from a stranger, so why me? But I will never forget that kindness." By the work of the Holy Spirit that person will someday know that it is Jesus' love because no other love exists in this world, only His. The most wonderful thing is that the love of God is eternal, it is vast, it is unfathomable, and it flows continually to this world.

Let's be part of passing it on, as our friend Joyce says, "The most important thing in life is to accept Jesus and keep a relationship with Him every day!" That simply is the love of Jesus.

"O what love, what boundless love
God has bestowed on me,
O what love, what boundless love
God has bestowed on me,
Calling me a child of God,
Planting my feet where the saints have trod,
Lifting me up to the realms above
O what boundless love."
-Philip Cameron/Roy Turner

To Him who sits on the throne and to the lamb, be blessing and honor and glory and dominion forever and ever and

Chapter Fourteen

Wonder

Quiet Thoughts on Wonder

Is it wrong to sit and wonder,
When my God is the Eternal,
Is the ever-living One?
When His mercy is unbounded
And His promise true and sure?
May I sit and gaze at Glory
Like the sunset ending day?

As I contemplate each day,
Keep me humble, help me pray.
With all my heart I want to yield:
Help me quietly wait and listen
To Thy Spirit. . .then obey.

And when the darkness seems to hover
O'er my thoughts - the path unclear -
Draw me to an upward look
To see the stars, reminders still
Of Thy wonders, strength and wisdom,
Joy and peace from Thine unending store.

231

Yes, 'Tis right to sit and wonder,
To ponder on Thy love and grace,
To spend with Thee these quiet moments,
As Thou to me Thyself unfold.
And so I'll gaze upon Thy Glory
'Till I see Thee face to Face.

*   *   *   *   *

Little Things Mean a Lot

If you are not singing what the title may suggest perhaps you will by the time you read what follows! Some of the words in the song are about diamonds and pearls, rings and other little things, but that's not what you will sing when you get to the finish! Jesus demonstrates a fondness for little things: The mustard seed, two coins, the sparrow, the kernel of wheat, and little children among many other little things. So we don't need to shy away from little things, instead let's focus for a while on little things. This will be a medley of ideas to muse on, things to remember, things to chew on, things out of the past, present, and all of them precious.

Butterfly Kisses: A flicker of love, gentle and sweet, between Grandpa and his little sweetheart; that's a butterfly kiss. The eye-lash on the cheek: What a dear fleeting touch to remember, quite precious, especially when Grandpa is no longer here to repeat the gesture, which speaks of love, kinship, and endearment.

A Thank-you Note: Written spontaneously for a routine duty. While walking into Dillard's one day, a shopper stopped us as she was exiting.

There was an unmistakable exclamation of joy! "I know you! Yes, I do."

She was so certain, but Shiona wasn't, until the lady explained herself.

Looking directly at Shiona, she repeated herself, "Yes, I know you. I am a nurse at North Kansas City Hospital. You came to the lab one day and I did the labs for you. It's quite a while back, but you did the kindest thing. You wrote me a thank-you note! I will never forget, in fact, I still have that note and I will always keep it. I am so glad to see you and to tell you how much it has meant to me!"

"That was probably three or four years ago," replied Shiona, still bewildered by the suddenness of this recognition. "I can't believe you still remember me; I wouldn't have known you except that you stopped me just now, but how happy I am that you did!"

It's good to remember,
It's good to look back,
It's good to say "Thank-you"
It's like a pat on the back!

A Friendship in Germany: This is a real friendship, one that leaves footprints in your heart! During our three years in Germany we had become very attached; meals together, trips together, games together, prayer together, Bible Study together, and walks together. I guess we thought ourselves related! These friends started their family in Germany, we were about ten years ahead of them. Yet the bonding happened. Now we know God brought us together for His pleasure and ours (Philippians 2:13 again). This army couple moved back home to Minnesota. We moved back to California. The years passed; there were a few visits across the miles. Isn't it a happy thing that friendship doesn't find mountains and prairies difficult to cross? Later, our family had moved to Oregon, then to New York, and finally to Kansas City. Their children grew, and they added more children to their clan while our clan became smaller. But as good friends do, they comforted.

Then one day the phone rang, "Hey, you guys, got news for you. How would you like it if we moved to Kansas City?"

Now that wasn't hard to take, we needed some "family" near us. God knew all about it.

He was there that Sunday morning in Germany when Ken and Jay said, "Hi, what's your name? Mine is Ken and this is Glenda."

"Well, I'm Jay and this is Janet."

Now, forty years later, our friendship has become almost next door. It's the little things like, "Glad to meet you," that get our Father's plan moving. Isn't our Father good? One day recently Ken and Glenda visited and brought their six-year-old granddaughter with them. Bella was full of excitement about the soon arrival of a baby sister.

"It's so nice for you to have another sister, Bella," Bella caught on that Shiona didn't have a sister.

So she answered, "But Shiona, the Bible talks about brothers and sisters so you can have a sister, too." Little children, so sweet, so loving; covering the need of the moment, with a few heart-warming words. Jesus loves them so!

A few small words of, "Hey, what's your name?" Then reaping a harvest of, "Let's get together." Or "We sure miss you."

I thank You, Father, for real friendships that knit us tightly to each other!

Jesus not only *uses* little things, but honors them, too: Two small coins, more worth, more meaning than the super chunk out of the rich man's hoard. A kernel of wheat, pushed into the ground dies, yet brings forth a 30, 60 or 100 fold harvest. I know we don't like to *die* in this "receiving manifold blessings" curriculum, but it's better to die now and live forever, than to hug the "good things" of the world and lose out on everlasting forgiveness, joy, and peace. Jesus places great value on us. He compares us to a sparrow that His Father sees and cares for, then says, "How much more valuable are you than a sparrow. Won't He care for and love you enormously more than the sparrow?" (Luke 12:6-7). So don't let the sparrow have an opportunity to say to the robin, "I think that these anxious human beings have no heavenly Father, such as cares for you and me."

The little (and big) worries that bend us almost to the ground: Did we forget that Jesus wore a crown of thorns? In the crown of thorns were the many worries we think we can manage on our own? He told us that thorns choke out the good Word. We don't want that to happen. Better to be feasting than frowning. One winter day I looked out the window and saw the sturdy oak tree heavily burdened with snow. Some branches were almost to the ground. Thinking to myself, *Someone needs to go out and help that tree,* but then my thoughts made a U-turn. Maybe I was subconsciously thinking about the worries I was carrying. A seemingly insignificant glimpse can take our thoughts right back to where they should be. Those worries were bending me over. I needed to take them right then to Jesus.

Whoever thought Your crown would be of twisted thorns You wore for me?

Thank You, dear Jesus!

A little bee, a desultory bee (a parable from the writings of Lilias Trotter, 1883-1928; missionary to North Africa): Instead of sending you to the dictionary here's the definition of desultory: Passing abruptly and irregularly from one thing to another; starting suddenly as if by a leap; not connected with what precedes.

Lilias writes: "A bee comforted me very much this morning concerning the desultoriness that troubles me in our work. There seems so infinitely much to be done, that nothing gets done thoroughly. If work were more concentrated, as it must be in educational or medical missions, there would be less of this, but we seem only to touch souls and leave them. And that was what the bee was doing, figuratively speaking. He was hovering among some blackberry sprays, just touching the flowers here and there in a very tentative way, yet all unconsciously, life-life-life was left behind at every touch, as the miracle-working pollen grains were transferred to the place where they could set the unseen spring working. We have only to see to it that we are surcharged, like the bees, with potential life. It is God and His eternity that will do the work. Yet He needs His wandering, desultory bees!"

So may we all take the life-producing Word of God and distribute it to whomever He sends us.

Thank You, dear Father, for You have given me a picture of my daughter as she goes about touching a life here and there as You give her the inspiration and impulse, the words and songs. Father, bless, I pray, all who are bold enough by Your Holy Spirit to spread abroad Your love, Your life, Your comfort, and Your peace. Bless those who are touched with a token of Your love. Thank You, Father, in Jesus name, Amen.

Silver bells and pomegranates: Open a pomegranate some day and see how it is put together. It contains quite a parable under its leathery, reddish purple skin; like a beautiful coat topped with a crown! It is a reminder of the scarlet robe and crown of thorns; now a canopy of protection. Break the fruit open and you will see families sitting together, separated by a thin membrane, from other families. Then look at those seed groupings, how each seed is fastened to the life-giving, thick white flesh that nourishes each seed until it is plump with real nourishment waiting just for you! Do you see a faint picture of the Church of Jesus Christ; His people gathered together in groups, but are they gathered together in unity? How marvelously they sit there, enjoying the touch of one another, growing together with ease. Each seed is so bright and colorful you could say they even sparkle with joy.

If a pomegranate could sing, it would sing aloud with joy. But we are those seeds, bright red, washed in the blood of the Lamb, feasting on Him in fellowship and communion. We together are singing His praises, singing aloud for joy yet ready to go out as seeds in the blessing of others. Reminds us of the early history of His Church—being sent out with seed!

Thank You, Father, for pomegranates, the fruit of seeds, and for joy!

In Exodus 28:33-34 we learn about the garments of the priests.

And you shall make on its hem pomegranates of blue and purple and scarlet material, all around on its hem, and bells of gold between them all around: a golden bell and a pomegranate, a golden bell and a pomegranate, all around on the hem of the robe.

Don't you think there was a good reason why the robes of the priests in the Old Testament were fringed with pomegranates and bells? We know about the care and precision the priests were concerned with when they went once yearly into the Holy Place. If there was anything amiss, in themselves or in their responsibilities, they would not come out alive and the absence of the sound of the bells would issue an alarm. Their garments were strikingly beautiful, and we know from scripture that fruit and music both play an important part in God's Word, and are a foretaste of what we will experience in our Home up above. Perhaps He would like to see us abound right now, in the fruit of the Spirit and singing the high praises to our Savior, exercising our privilege in music, praise, and joy to His honor and pleasure. Now, let's sing!

Praise ye the Lord. From the rising of the sun till the going down of the same our Lord's name is to be praised. Praise ye the Lord, praise Him all ye servants of the Lord. (Psalm 113:1, 3)

*   *   *   *   *

Fringes of His Ways
Embraced by the Holy One

"The fringes of His ways," (Job 26:7-14 NASB) enumerates the exhibition of God's almighty power. He talks of the vastness of the universe, how God stretches out the north over empty space, and hangs the earth on nothing. He continues to tell of the boundary of light and darkness, and that the pillars of heaven tremble, being amazed at His rebuke. He quiets the sea, and by His breath the heavens are made beautiful. Think of that while looking at a sunrise or sunset, and at blue skies and white billowy clouds. Then we must bow and take a few deep breaths, as we read: "Behold, these are the fringes of His ways." Only the fringes, the borders or margins of His Ways!

I love the story of the woman who said to herself, "If I can only touch the fringe of His garment, I will be healed" (Luke 8:43-48 NASB). It is likely that she hoped only to get that close. But that touch to the fringe of His robe brought her right into His embrace. She was hoping that she would not be noticeable while carefully edging her way through the crowd of people who always seemed to be surrounding Jesus. Perhaps, on second thought she would slip away, *Ah, but I have tried everything; my need is too great.* Nor did Jesus fail to notice her. She only touched the fringe of His garment and He knew. He knew her need and her longing. The beauty of Jesus' response to her, a sick and needy one with a flow of blood making her an untouchable, surely causes us to pause and wonder. Yet Jesus came for such, and He would not ignore her. She was not to be unnoticed by the Son of God, who is also Son of Man; the One touched by the feelings of our infirmities and our weaknesses. He is the Almighty, the glorious, unspotted One.

There is therefore now no longer any condemnation. For the law was given through Moses; (to keep lepers far away and even a woman with a flow of blood); *while grace and truth came by Jesus Christ.* (Romans 8:1; John 1:17)

"Daughter," He called her, indicating a family relationship, which was saying, "I know you, and I want you to know Me!" Then He said, "Your faith has made you whole!" No longer was she untouchable, no longer alone, no longer on the outside looking in. She was enfolded in His embrace. She belonged now to Him. She came with no friend, now Jesus was her Friend. The One who is the Creator was now her intimate Savior. She was now in the circle of His favor, in the circle of the Father's love. The Almighty One touched her life. This encounter was only the beginning, the fringe, the edge, the border; for now she was clothed in the garment of salvation and the robe of His righteousness. These would be her new wardrobe, as she walked in a new Way. How well He knows us. I think that these words from Psalm 139 were some of her thoughts that day and the days following.

O Lord, Thou has searched me and known me. . . and art intimately acquainted with all my ways. . .Thou has enclosed me behind and before and laid Thy hand upon me. . .Thy hand will lead me. . . Wonderful are Thy works. . . How precious also are Thy thoughts to me, O God. . .How vast the sum of them!. . . .Lead me in the everlasting Way!"

She whispers as she hugs herself, "You have called me Daughter!" We meet the Savior at the fringes of His ways, but wonder is wrapped up in these fringes. We cannot fathom His ways, for they are everlasting and holy. But wonder keeps us pushing to know more of the One who loves us so. We come up against the Word that says, "As for God His way is perfect" (Psalm 18:30), and passed finding out. Yet He says to us, "This is the way, walk ye in it" (Isaiah 18:31 KJV). Only He knows the Way and He shows us the Way, because His love encompasses our whole life.

O how He love us, and the invitation is simple enough, "Come unto Me and I will give you rest!" (Matthew 11:28). Like the woman in the story we also are embraced by the Holy One, when we have pushed past the crowd of anxious thoughts and fearsome threats and touched the fringe! *Thank You, Lord Jesus.*

Bring us farther and farther beyond the mere fringes of Your ways, Lord Jesus. And some day we will be in that place where there will be no end to our knowing You. That will be the place of our eternal Home, so we pray, "Even so, come, Lord Jesus, Come!" (Revelation 22:20 KJV)

* * * * *

What Is This Life?

Called to serve by doing nothing?

Called to serve by only waiting?
Called to serve by sitting still?
Yes! Called to serve the living King.

Dashed the hopes that lay asleep,
Crushed desires. . .were they all wrong?
Hurried minutes now seem to mock.
Gone those moments, days and hours.

Take me back, Lord, to those hours
When You spoke encouraging words.
Take me to the table spread,
Bid me eat of heavenly Bread.

In Your image we were made -
Yet in our own choices, we went our way.
But You installed Redemption's Plan
To bring us back: We'd be a clan.

Broken, crushed, we hid away.
But Christ was ever on that path
That led uphill to Calvary Mount;
Outside, outside - nor friend was near.

The Father's face far-hidden, now
Jesus alone under lashes did bow,
His head, His hands, His feet, for me.
And now His side must pierc'ed be.

The call goes forth, "My Son, My Son,
My beloved Son now crucified,
Buried, now raised to life again.
You'll bring them Home by Your strong arm."

So what the waiting, so much undone.

So what the hours of sitting still.
The selfish hopes, and crushed desires
Amount to nothing in worship's hours.

Looking up and not around
Brings to focus One glory-crowned.
My cares I'll exchange for peace tonight;
For secret treasures and songs in the night.

Alone, away, just standing still
Yet serving Him in a small quiet place;
In that hidden place Him adorn,
Laying all before Him at the Throne.

*   *   *   *   *

I Have Chosen You!

Chosen

> To belong to Him
> To be clay in His hand

Chosen

> For His pleasure
> For His glory
> For His purpose
> For fellowship with the Father,
> With the Son, with the Holy Spirit

Chosen

> To be forgiven
> To be humble

To be willing
To be emptied
To be filled
To be sanctified
To be His child
To be fellow-workers
To be perfected in unity
To be light and salt
To be glorified

Chosen

To honor Him
To worship Him
To love Him
To praise Him
To talk with Him
To listen to Him
To live for Him
To love one another
To receive grace

Chosen

For this time
For this place
For these joys
For this grief or sorrow
For these gifts
For these treasures
For these duties or distresses

Chosen

To shine

To rest
To believe
To obey
To trust
To soar
To climb
To reflect my Father's love

You did not choose Me, but I chose you, and appointed you, that you should go and bear fruit, and that your fruit should remain. (John 15:16)

BY FAITH Abraham lived as an alien in the LAND of PROMISE dwelling in tents --- for he was looking for the city which has foundations, whose ARCHITECT and BUILDER is GOD. Heb 11:9-10

Chapter Fifteen

Land of Promise

To Live Beyond-Above

To live beyond-above the turmoil,
The enemy would not have it so.
But, I belong to Christ, my Savior, to Him will I go.

To live beyond-above the chaos of the day,
O Savior, step between my heart and ways
that would offend.
For I belong to Jesus, my Fortress and my Friend.

To live beyond-above the wounds, the hurts.
Bruised hearts, dark, clouded eyes,
Hold gently in Your scarred Hand. . .none more
near, nor wise.

To live beyond-above careless, flying words,
Word of God incarnate, illuminate, saturate
My heart, my mind with comforting words of
Love. Dominate!

247

To live beyond-above a selfish, narrow thought,
That could with blundering tongue wound another's smile;
I'd rather learn from You, dear Savior, to go another mile!

To live beyond-above disturbance with courage
and good cheer;
Thou Son of God for certain joy the rugged cross endured
Grand welcome waits in heavenly courts - our eternal
life ensured.

To live beyond-above is possible in this realm,
For Jesus made the way and now exclaims, "Do not fear!"
"Courage take with joy; in weakness, I am strong,
always near!"

*   *   *   *   *

The Faith-Walk

Growing up with near-sightedness made glasses much more than an option; they were a necessity. My mother was far-sighted, and secretly I would rather have had her eyes than mine, because everything faraway was very clear to her, but fuzzy to me. When I first got glasses, I remember exclaiming the wonders of seeing that leaves on trees had sharply cut outlines. For me this was the eighth wonder of the world. It was finally exciting to look around at the accurately defined world of nature. Everything was so especially distinct. What a joy to look out on the world!

Far-sightedness definitely has an advantage over short-sightedness. Recently, rereading a book by V. Raymond Edman, I took special note of his closing comment on the subject of sight, "With far-sightedness we walk by Faith." How well put! I readily agree with him. Far-sightedness speaking spiritually can take us beyond and above; *beyond* the circumstances of the here and now, and *above* to the Throne of God and His grace and wisdom.

Where does near-sightedness take us? No farther than our toenails and with much stumbling! In fact sight, without faith, is near-sighted because we rationalize, "I can do this" or "I'll say it my way" or the big one "I will!" or "I will not!" It's all about *me*. But when push comes to shove, we are scared. "Where's God! He's supposed to help *me*." Oh yeah, even when you made the decisions and plans all by yourself? Thankfully, He never says, "No, I'm too busy." Rather He will wrap us in His love until we can listen and learn His way.

In Genesis 22, Abraham spoke far-sighted faith to his son. How else could he answer Isaac's question, "My father, here is the fire and the wood, but where is the lamb for the burnt offering?" I'm sure Abraham's heart had done its flip-flops long before this moment. We are not told the many walks and talks he had with God before this moment arrived. He was given the magnificent gift of faith from God. We know that faith in God is not natural to us. Like David, Abraham strengthened himself in his faith and could lead his son right up to the final moment of testing.

Out of that faith he could say with conviction, "My son, God will provide Himself a lamb." It was the Lamb of God, Jesus in a pre-incarnate appearance, who spoke out, "Abraham, Abraham, do not stretch out your hand against the lad, and do nothing to him, for now I know that you fear God." Abraham obeyed and God responded. Look! There's a ram caught in the bushes! The sacrifice for the burnt offering was already there, waiting. The reward of faith is to find out that our Father already has provision made for us. He waits for us to wait on Him and trust Him.

In Hebrews 11:1 it says, "Now faith is the assurance (substance) of things hoped for, the evidence (conviction) of things not seen." I see in the above narrative the substance and conviction (or assurance and evidence) of Abraham's faith when he was able to say to his son, "God will provide" even in that final moment when he lifted up his knife to slay his son. At this point there was no lamb. Abraham's far-sighted spiritual eyes saw that the Lamb was provided; that God's promise of Isaac's seed was not going to be terminated that day. His faith was greatly strengthened in his obedience.

Yes, Jesus trusts us to trust Him—what a marvel! He is the Rock, He is the Fortress, He is the Stronghold. Wait a minute, does He have a *strong hold* on you? Do you allow Him and do you always look to Him? Our faith can grow. It grows by reading His Word, by praying, by waiting, and by listening. With each little bit you feel He is telling you, go ahead and step out on that little stepping stone just in front of you. See what God will do!

*   *   *   *   *

"I'm going to make spaghetti," Shiona said as she was planning her day.

She had made a few steps forward in rehabilitation, but I wasn't sure about this idea of spaghetti making. I stayed nearby, probably hovering, and making a few comments.

She said, "It's okay, Mom, Jesus is helping me. He knows what to do."

Sitting on the kitchen stool trying to keep my distance, I watched, and decided a comment would be okay. In fact I thought it was urgent!

"Maybe that's too much water, Shiona."

"No, it isn't. I'm okay, 'cause Jesus is telling me what to do."

Then a few minutes later she said, "Here's the only thing you can do. Call around and find a homeless shelter that needs some dinner tonight."

Uh-Oh! This was the second surprise - find some hungry folks! What do you do when you know she's really saying, "Mom, don't hover. This is *my* business."

So I stayed in my corner with the phone in my hand, and a prayer in my heart, "O Lord, make this work. I don't think she made it right, too much water, and she threw the pasta right into the pot of thin, watery sauce. It's all one big pot of soupy food. I know she put in herbs - but how much? I don't know if she measured the salt and pepper. Well, Lord, You are in charge of this, please make it taste right, and provide the folks that need it."

Yeah, it sounds like I was worrying! I got out the telephone book. I knew of one shelter where we had been taking lunches a few years previously, and called their number.

"Hello," said the manager of the shelter.

"By any chance, could you use some food tonight?" I asked. "I know it is getting close to dinner time, but we could bring something."

"Yes, we sure can use some dinner tonight. I don't have anything to feed my people but a few sandwiches. What time will you be here?"

"Oh, in about an hour, I think, better let me ask the chef!"

It wasn't very long when Shiona announced, "Look, it's all ready!"

A quick peek into the pot told me it actually smelled and looked like the real thing!

Likewise a quick taste said, "It's good, they will enjoy it!"

I shouldn't be surprised or should I? Wow! She did it! I talked to the Lord for a few minutes, "Thank You, Jesus. You answered her prayer." Yes, I am sure she was praying, so was I.

"They will enjoy it, Shiona. Hope they're real hungry," I said as I settled my jitters.

A half hour drive got us into downtown Kansas City. There was parking right in front of the house.

"I'm sure it's heavy. Can you carry it?" I asked because it was my biggest stainless steel soup pot.

"Yes, I can carry it. Please don't worry. Mom, you seem awfully nervous."

The front door opened, "Oh, my, here you are. How wonderful. I needed this tonight, as I honestly didn't know what to feed them. Food is short and the fridge is almost empty. Come on into the kitchen. Oh, it smells so good. Thank you so very much! Let me put it in something else, as I am sure you want to take your pot back," said the worker.

Then came Shiona's quick reply, "Oh, no, the pot is yours. You keep it."

Surprise number three! She just gave away my biggest soup pot!

"Are you sure?" insisted the worker.

"Oh, yes, that's yours to keep," was Shiona's very happy response. She loves to give!

I will admit to thinking, "My biggest soup pot, I need that pot! No, Shiona, please don't." But, thank God, I didn't say a word.

Later while relating her fantastic day, her Dad took a moment to respond to me, "Honey, there are more ways to give. Go buy yourself a pot!"

This was to be a never forgotten day! She was so excited, having been able to feed that houseful of homeless people *and Jesus was there to help her.* She also did it without Mom hovering (very much)! We both began learning things that day. We learned to start all over again. Many things got lost in the long hospitalization, resulting in the mental dysfunction that Shiona suffered through.

Her Dad and I were alarmed at all that was lost to her, and then how to regain stable functioning for all of us. We sought to recapture equilibrium in the day to day routines of life. This was an ever-present concern. But didn't God show that He was with us?

Most important, Shiona needed a lot of support in her spiritual life. Did God still love her? Did He really forgive her sins? We went over and over the promises in His Word that she *really* belonged to Him, and that He would never leave her nor forsake her. This "spaghetti day" was a day to prove that He was there to help her. How many, many times after this day I could sense the same proving was going on in her mind and activities. Simply reaching out to people wherever she was came to be the same testing place. It was like getting into the swimming pool one toe at a time to make sure the water temperature is right. It was a growing back into the comfort zone of God's love and care.

A "broken brain" leaves immense insecurity when the episode begins to heal and hospitalization is a thing of the past. The emotional and spiritual needs had to be dealt with gently and kindly, with lots of patience and understanding. I think that for Shiona these were days of re-grasping her faith; for learning again that we are protected by the shield of faith. For us *standing still* beside her we are told in 1 Thessalonians 5:14, "Encourage the fainthearted (Moffat), comfort those who are frightened" (which is a common symptom after hospitalizations), "comfort the timid or those of sinking hearts (Way) and soothe them of little soul."(Rotherham) All of these various ways of putting the thought across have helped us when we've faced the differing moods or outlooks of someone struggling back to "normal."

Faith always has new areas to conquer; however when we walk with far-sightedness we are equipped to see; really see, as Abraham did.

By faith, when he was called, obeyed by going out to a place which he was to receive for an inheritance; and he went out, not knowing where he was going. . . By faith he lived as an alien in the land of promise, as in a foreign land, dwelling in tents with Isaac and Jacob, fellow-heirs of the same promise; for he was looking for the city which has foundations whose architect and builder is God. (Hebrews 11:8, 10)

I like to reread the story of Abraham, it seems to fit our lives. Think of these things in the above quotation:

- called
- obeyed
- not knowing
- an alien
- yet promises abound
- an inheritance coming
- this dilemma is like a foreign land
- living in a tent because this life is only a temporary habitation

We are only living in view of the grand and glorious future God has planned for us. Yes, it is worth the distress, disaster, the dread of the diagnoses, and anything else we could add to the list. It is encouraging to go back again and again to read about Abraham's life and take another far-sighted look. Believe me, it looks good! Again my heart refers back to the message in the dream, "Whatever difficulty you face, it is worth the struggle, the pain, and the disappointment."

* * * * *

Blessings

Blessings because He loves me.
Blessings still to come.
But 'tis true, I know it's true.
Because, He without sparing gave all.

He opens His hand and graciously gives,
He graciously gives to all.

By taking all from His loving hand,
Then from His hand will come
That good He has promised in all things;
All things for the good of His own.
He opens His hand and graciously gives,
He graciously gives to all.

None there is who pleads in vain;
He answers every call.
For faithful is He in all He does,
As He graciously gives and gives.
He opens His hand and graciously gives,
He graciously gives to all.

We have all benefited from the rich blessings He brought to us - blessing upon blessing heaped upon us. (John 1:16 TLB)

Thou givest. . . they gather. You open Your hand, they are filled with good. (Psalm 104:28 KJV)

* * * * *

Navigating the Wilderness

When the wilderness blooms it is because Jesus is there! Have you ever seen the desert in bloom? It is a beautiful sight. It is full of color; the reds, corals, oranges, and lavenders blending as lovely as a sunset, and very striking against the neutral color of the sand. That the desert blooms means there has been plenty of rain, showers of blessing *in the desert*. But the beauty of the desert or wilderness is short-lived. So it is good that also in the wilderness where our trials may take us, there is a secret place, a prepared place where is found nourishment.

Can we even question that we live in the wilderness? When we read and re-read the Old Testament isn't there a parallel to our lives? The Israelites didn't like the wilderness. But God says it was to test them, and the many who rebelled never got into the Promised Land. Likewise we are not yet living in the Promised Land; that is still coming. But we have many, many promises while living in this wilderness.

After Jesus was baptized by John, He was led into the wilderness by the Spirit and was tempted by Satan. Jesus overcame, not just in the wilderness, but in His whole life He overcame. At the climax of His mission He overcame on the cross for us and rose again. Now in the wilderness of this life we possess His Life in us by the Holy Spirit, the Comforter. We have comfort in the wilderness.

And the woman (believers) *fled into the wilderness where she had a place prepared by God, so that there she might be nourished.* (Revelation 12:6).

I like how Elizabeth Clephane expresses this thought in her hymn:

"Beneath the cross of Jesus, I fain would take my stand,
The shadow of a mighty rock within a weary land;
A home within the wilderness, a rest upon the way,
From the burning of the noon-tide heat, and the burden
of the day."

To tell the truth, we don't like the wilderness. Sometimes we pretend that we do, and we gather material stuff around us for comfort, but when the trials come we know we are still in the wilderness because our comfort stuff doesn't add up to our expectations. Gradually, or it could happen all at once, we are stripped of all or almost all our stuff; as in a tornado, serious illness, bad economy or an unwanted intrusion. It's good to stop right then and humbly, before the Father, confess our feeble efforts. Instead, we should have been leaning on Him and taking from His hand while appreciating the comfort that has been prepared for us from before all the "befores."

It occurs to me that the wilderness is not a place where you would want to be alone. We know it to be a lonely place. I have been in the desert, the dry and dusty place where there is no water, no shade, and neither refreshing. Trying to make that journey alone is deathlike, frightful, and downright scary. It tests and weakens even the strongest. Crossing the desert in times past was a real test of bravery.

In the early days of automobile travel, the driver would have to navigate a road that consisted only of two ribbons of wooden planks laid separately end-to-end for right and left tires. This went on for miles. Getting off the plank highway was something you didn't want to have happen. I'm sure many folks would rather have had a camel! You've probably heard old family desert stories that take you to the edge of disaster.

Out of my family's history came this story of being on the "plank highway" through Arizona. They did have unexpected car trouble and Grandpa had to walk back to the last scrap of a town to find a mechanic. Meanwhile Grandma, being Scottish, had a hankering for a "wee cuppa tea." Uncle George was sent to find a few dry sticks and make a fire. A bit of precious water went into the sterling silver teapot. Alas, before the tea was ready you can guess what happened to the precious teapot! It melted into a silver ingot. But God is good, there was not much money left, and behold, the mechanic got the car started, and got paid with a mound of silver! God preserves us even in the desert. (By the way the twenty-year old driver was my mother: A first driving lesson that became a cross-country excursion!)

The particular kind of wilderness experience confronting our family came glaring out at me from the pages of a book by a favorite author. I was reading about the gift our Lord has given us in the Body of Christ. The scripture she used was the familiar Hebrews 10:25, "Not forsaking the assembling of ourselves together, as is the manner of some, but exhorting one another, and so much the more as you see the Day approaching."

My immediate reaction was sadness because for such a long time our family had been feeling isolated because of what our daughter was going through physically, emotionally, and mentally. I thought, *If this is a wonderful gift from our Father, why can't everyone experience and benefit from the Body of Christ?* While absorbing the author's thoughts, I was writing in the margin of the book, "I feel so saddened by this." So I stopped my reading, spent some time thinking, and asking the Lord to help me with this.

It is, indeed, a sad message for someone who is on the outside looking in because there are circumstances that can't be helped or that require attendance and you cannot step away from the duty. Jesus had not shown me clearly how to handle this. I had been struggling with it, and for too long feeling tension in myself. I don't like struggle and would rather be at peace. But God is never late! The fellowship we enjoyed seemed to be sliding a little more out of reach, like a ship leaving its mooring is drawn farther and farther out to sea and is soon past the horizon. But instead it was our family that was slipping away from fellowship. The fellowship group was still there, but we weren't.

I had read about Samuel Rutherford, exiled to the dreary north of Scotland, restricted in his associations to letters written to his parishioners at home in Anwoth in the south of Scotland. Being denied the return to his Anwoth parish, he says, "Anwoth is not heaven, preaching is not Christ." So for his desired fellowship he must wait, but his letters are filled with his satisfaction with His Savior, His love, and His nearness. He was indeed experiencing a wilderness trial, a trial of isolation. However, in God's providence we cannot begin to measure the good that has come from his testimony in the form of letters and encouragements. Some of his letters have become hymns that we have sung in churches for the last several hundred years. The words and teaching inherent in these hymns linger on. A good example is Rutherford's hymn that will be recognized by many Christians:

> "The sands of time are sinking,
> The dawn of heaven breaks,
> The summer morn I've sighed for,
> The fair sweet morn awakes.
> Dark, dark hath been the midnight,
> But dayspring is at hand,
> And glory, glory dwelleth,
> In Emmanuel's land."

Can't you feel the comfort in those few lines?

I recall reading one day where Paul said, "Remember to pray for those in prison as though you were there with them" (Hebrews13:3). Being isolated for any reason or in any circumstance brings with it the acute feeling of aloneness. I understood this well when Shiona was in isolation at the beginning of a serious hospitalization. Isolation is a word that is filled with negative feeling. We by nature do not want to be isolated. If we experience it, it seems to me, it must be thrust upon us.

Perhaps one reason why God allows that experience to come to us is so that we can intercede more earnestly and more willingly for those who are in prison, isolated or home-bound for whatever reason. Madam Guyon and John Bunyan are also among many who show us how God uses the trial of isolation. There are many recent stories of isolation because of belief in Jesus, testimonies of persons under persecution.

Then another thought came to me from Hebrews 12:1 which says, "We are surrounded by so great a cloud of witnesses." Who might these witnesses be? Reading so many books of Amy Carmichael has caused me to think of her as a friend. She always has an encouraging word for me. I can also mention Ruth Myers and her many helpful books, also Mrs. C. E. Cowman and her devotional books. Going back often to these writers, though they are not here now, is like visiting with old friends. Even contemporary writers become friends, though I haven't talked to many, but they, too, are ones I fellowship with in reading their books or articles. They are talking to me, and if we were face to face, we would have quite a discussion about some things, I am sure.

It is often said that books are friends. I like to think that the authors are my friends, folks I go to often, but not by telephone or a visit at Panera's, but to my bookshelf. After all, we have learned this from Jesus who is the Word. We know He talks to us through His Word, which surpasses any book, old or new. Then there are others like C. H. Spurgeon, A. W. Tozer, Andrew Murray, Hudson Taylor, and on and on the list of friends goes. Neither will we forget our Bible friends. I'm sure we all often think about the time coming when we will actually sit down with them and ask many, many questions, never having to say, "I guess my time is up, I've kept you long enough!"

These are some things that help frighten away my sad thoughts on the days that I want so badly some person-to-person fellowship. In these times of e-communication I think that we can slide more and more into a practice of not having the kind of fellowship that our parents and grandparents experienced in their Christian walk and life in the Body of Christ. Face-to-face meeting with a friend is something very special, something I long for. Nevertheless, there is always a reason for the circumstances that we encounter.

We must believe with our whole heart that these occasions have God's reasons at the root of them. He is teaching us, sometimes to teach others, sometimes to bring us to the maturity that He desires for us. If we can lay it all on the altar, on Jesus and rest in Him and on Him, we can freely enjoy this part of our journey. We are journeying with Him to the Home He has prepared for us. In that Home we will never experience a wilderness ever again.

But for now my Beloved offers streams in the desert, offers His presence in the desert, the cloud of His presence which gives the shade, and a way of escape for every temptation. In the wilderness of no help, no resource; He is the Source. Without Him the lonely traveler would die. But He is my Beloved and His desire is for me. It is not good to try to live without Him, because this world *is* a wilderness. "Who is this coming up from the wilderness, leaning on her Beloved?" (Song of Solomon 8:5). It is the one who has found her Beloved Savior and Friend, the Lord Jesus Christ, her source and nourishment in the desert.

The Lord is God, there is no one else. (1 Kings 8:6)

There is an interesting story in Genesis about a woman named Hagar (Genesis 21:8-14). She bore Abraham a son, but he was not the promised son. She was also Sarah's maid, but Sarah found fault with her. Becoming jealous, she asked Abraham to send her away. So Hagar left the tent of Abraham and wandered in the wilderness, but presently sat down by a spring of water. That is where the Angel of the Lord found her, by a spring of water! But it also says He had to open her eyes to see it.

When I read this story it always says something to me, such as: I wonder if when I find myself in a wilderness experience that the Lord, when He looks for me, will find me by a spring of water—the Spring of Everlasting Water! That is the water that Jesus says He will give to those who are thirsty. Jesus says that whoever desires may "come and take the Water of Life freely" (Revelation 22:17). He is the only Source for those of us who are thirsty. He knows our need of refreshment, support, and strengthening. Sometimes we can find ourselves not drinking at the Well of His Word. We need to pay attention to our thirst daily. Sometimes what God has asked us to do in our life seems just too much. Nothing, it seems gets better, progress seems to be in regression instead of improving. The endurance required reminds me of a poem by Amy Carmichael. I have read it many, many times and I offer it to you:

The Age-long Minute

"Thou art the Lord who, slept upon the pillow,
Thou art the Lord who, soothes the furious sea.
What matter beating wind and tossing billow
If only we are in the boat with Thee?

Hold us in quiet through the Age-long Minute
While Thou art silent, and the wind is shrill.
Can the boat sink while Thou, dear Lord, art in it?
Can the heart faint that waiteth on Thy will?"

The Age-long Minute, what does that mean? Is it when we think God has forgotten all about us and all we can think is, "I've had enough, no more, please, God. Change these circumstances!" He would like us to change our viewpoint and see as He sees, that this "momentary light affliction is working for us a far more exceeding and eternal weight of glory" (2 Corinthians 4:17). We sing heartily, "It will be worth it all when we see Jesus," but are we singing it with meaning or in anguish?

After forty years of desert living, God told Moses he was standing on Holy Ground—in the desert, away from his family and God's people? Yes! He didn't have to move an inch or even to a different part of the desert, and he didn't have to go back to Egypt to his fellow Israelites. Right there in the *desert* he was standing on Holy Ground. "Take off your sandals, Moses!" That is victory in the desert! He is Emmanuel, God with us. He is with us in our wilderness, in the desert sand storm, the howling wind, and the tempest that cannot destroy Him. It cannot destroy me. I am in His company. I am standing on Holy Ground right here, right now!

We were in the car one day. I could feel discouragement coming on and started talking about this Holy Ground. Soon Shiona and I were singing together:

We are standing on Holy Ground,
We are standing on Holy Ground,
Though the crowd may pass us by,
We are standing on Holy Ground.

The words are ours (we can't find this in any of our hymn books) and you will have to make up your own tune! But the words sure help in those down moments!

Finally we crown Him Lord of All, because He teaches us in the desert. We learn that, yes, we will go through this with Him, not on our own. We learn to endure, for endurance has great reward. We learn to be away from the busyness of life around us, and how to live being loved and being nurtured by the Lord Jesus. Confident of doing His will, we can even forget the loneliness. He teaches us to look anew at our life and the glory we can give to Him in *all things*.

After all, Jesus was content when He said He had nowhere to lay His head. His sandals, tunic, and robe were enough for Him. He did not own a home, even though this world was made by Him. I often think of Him enclosed by a multitude so constantly. Then He would slip quietly away to the Mount of Olives, spending time alone with His Father. In the morning, refreshed, probably without much sleep, He would be ready again for the multitudes.

Can we also find the same refreshment in lonely moments that are placed in our day, perhaps just for His reasons? In this desert He has many things He would teach us. Let's be teachable and know that standing on Holy Ground is the only safe place. It is safe ground even when the wilderness is where we live. Isn't He the only navigator for this wilderness walk of ours? Even in our wilderness wandering, there will be showers of blessing. There will be the blessing of knowing that our Beloved's love for us is more beautiful than the desert blooming like a sunset!

The wilderness and the desert will be glad, and the desert will rejoice and blossom; like the crocus it will blossom profusely, and will rejoice with rejoicing and shouts of joy. . . They will see the glory of the Lord, the majesty of our God. Encourage the exhausted, strengthen the feeble. (Isaiah 35:2-3)

*   *   *   *   *

Thus Far

Is this the way He meant for me?
Have all these years passed as a vapor?
Does He call me by my name?
Have I by grace found His favor?

I'll answer "Yes" and say "Amen."
His ways are past my understanding.

My steps are written in His book;
His voice in my youth always calling. . .

. . ."I'll be with you in the struggle,
Shedding light along the way.
Up the mountain, one more step,
And take My joy for each new day."

"I have called you by your name,
And through this life I'll call you 'friend.'
Call on Me and I will answer.
I am with you to the end."

Our life, it touches but the fringes
Of His lofty thoughts and ways.
'Tis best, by faith, we keep on trusting,
Till we rise above this haze.

Even to your old age, I shall be the same and even to
your graying years I shall bear you! I have done it, and
I shall carry you and I shall bear you, and I shall deliver
you. (Isaiah 46:4)

Therefore do not lose heart, but though our outer man
is decaying, yet our inner man is being renewed day by
day. (2 Corinthians 4:16)

His commandment is eternal life. (John 12:50)

EVERYONE THEN WHO HEARS THESE WORDS
OF MINE AND ACTS ON THEM WILL BE LIKE
A WISE MAN WHO BUILT HIS HOUSE ON ROCK

Matt
7:24

Chapter Sixteen

The Master Builder

The Master Builder

Every house is built by someone, but the builder of all things is God. (Hebrews 3:4)

G od is the Master Builder. We are building, but not just our own plan and design.

What kind of material are we gathering together for our building? When we were children we built with sand, mud, grass, and sticks. It could happen when neighbor kids, the dog, the ducks, and chickens came along we would have to start all over. Our preparation was for nothing and we lost it all. We even felt worse if the building was about finished and sudden intruders destroyed all our work. Or it could happen on the sandy beach; who could control the tide? This is all childhood adventure. What about real life? We are all building and I am what I build so I need to build carefully. I need to build under the direction and supervision of the Master Builder.

Jesus talks plainly about the foundation for building. "The house on the sand went flat, but the house on the Rock stood firm" (Matthew 7:24-27). Only under the supervision of the Master Builder is it true that I will build a house that will stand when difficulties come.

Dear Father, I pray that I build according to the Pattern, that I follow the instruction Book, and keep close to You, the Master Builder. Help me, Lord, in all my ways, all my doings, in all my days, and all my hours, that what I build is built on the Rock, the sure Foundation. In doing the work and building, help me rest in the security of all Your building provisions. You are the Creator, the Architect, the Provider, and the Redeemer. You, and none other, are the Builder of ALL THINGS. I praise Your Name, Amen.

For who is God besides the Lord? (1 Corinthians 3:9)

And who is the Rock (foundation) except our God? (Psalm 18:31)

Except the Lord build the House, they labor in vain that build it. (Psalm 127:1)

We have a building from God, a house not made with hands, eternal in the heavens. (2 Corinthians 5:1)

Every house is built by someone, but the builder of all things is God. (Hebrews 3:4)

All Thy works shall praise Thee. (Psalm 145:10)

Commit your works to the Lord and your plans will be established. (Proverbs 16:3)

The mind of man plans his way, but the Lord directs his steps. (Proverbs 16:9)

*   *   *   *   *

God's Work: Philippians 2:13
To will and to do of His good pleasure.

In your personal Bible study have you come across what Paul says in Philippians 2:13? "For it is God who is at work in you both to will and to do of His good pleasure." Maybe, like me, you have stored it away, and pulled it out of your memory scroll from time to time, chewing on it and wondering: How does this work?

It was many years ago, I was still a teenager, and the prayer meeting was not very interesting. I opened my Bible and began reading Philippians. When I got to 2:13, I stopped and I read it again and again, again and again. Over and over I read the passage emphasizing the words in turn: It is *God*, who is at *work;* God who is at work in *me;* God who is at work in me to *will*; etc. I think you get the point. It was a revelation to think that God, Almighty God, was working in me. Then the remainder of the prayer meeting was spent meditating on this thought over and over in my mind. I didn't have the life experience yet to fully understand, but that verse has been with me all these years, coming back repeatedly, waiting for me to start seeing how the meaning truly would be revealed in real life.

Undoubtedly, being a teenager meant I needed to live longer to experience God at work in me. I was at first base, I was saved but peace is born through struggle later I could express it like this:

What is this work of God?
For me it's to believe
The Son receive
My burden relieve
And the work is done in Heav'n.
The work is passed
I wonder . . ."Alas,
'Tis simple to believe!"

But as many as received Him, to them He gave the right to become children of God, even to those who believe in His name. Jesus said, "This is the work of God, that you believe in Him whom He has sent." (John 1:12; 6:29)

Soon we find we are enrolled in His school: The place of learning His will and finding Him at work in our desires. As we compare God's will to our will, we know it doesn't measure up. The alarm rings in our spirit. Our will is not His will! In some ways we are still feasting on at least some of our own desires, and looking forward to our accomplishments. How would His will become my will, and how would His doing become my doing? Maybe that's when we "stumble" onto Philippians 2:13. Are all things that I am being taught according to *His pleasure*? That is a big question in a young person's mind.

For some kids in Christian College, it seemed so easy for them to say, "Well, such and such didn't happen, so God doesn't want me to do that." To me it didn't always seem that clear. Once a fellow student said to me, "I missed the street car connection, so that means the job interview was not God's will." Perhaps she was just slow that morning and didn't get her act together. At the same time, who am I to judge? Leave it alone!

Let's face it. For some people that we have read about, the teaching of our Lord in them was swift and to the point. I think of John and Betty Stam, martyred in China only a very few years after leaving Moody Bible Institute. Both John's and Betty's testimonies were clear and distinct, giving over their personal desires to the Lord in no uncertain words, while very young. Their first and only child was still an infant when the Communists came for them. They left their two month old baby wrapped in her sleeping bag on a bed in the place where John and Betty had been confined until their execution. First John, then Betty went swiftly to Jesus. Two days later, a Chinese Christian Pastor miraculously found the baby and delivered her to the grieving grandparents, who were missionaries in another part of China. She was still warm, but I am sure, hungry. God knew and God worked in John and Betty's lives, even to the utmost care of their new baby. They yielded quietly and quickly and after a very short lifetime went home glorifying Jesus.

Our son was quite sure that the next two years of his life would see him finishing Bible College and perhaps a year or so later on his way to Europe to minister with his pastor friend in Yugoslavia. It was not to be. Yes, God had been preparing him in specific ways for His specific reasons, but not to go to Europe, nor to marry his sweetheart. Robert is not here to answer questions about Philippians 2:13, but the evidence is in his journal of God's preparation. Robert's will was changed in his life, and his doings and goals were changed. These changes happened in the last two years of his life. Perhaps a short perusal of his journal will point out how Philippians 2:13 worked in his young life.

*　*　*　*　*

Between March 1977 and February 1978 is when these changes were happening. He went Home to Jesus August 10, 1978. He was nineteen. He begins his journal restating his relationship with Jesus: First, as. . .

". . .a distant relative for many years, but recently He and I have become best friends. I know He wants my life and I have given my life to Him for any purpose that would be of His benefit. This was a hard thing to finally resolve."

He notes that his "many interests and desires would take a lifetime of pursuing and never scratch the surface of intention."

Then he retells to himself of these things realizing that "all is fruitlessness, emptiness, and of no importance when one considers the vastness of eternity. . ."

Then he continues, "I therefore, lay down these areas as focal points and have determined to use all of my energies in pursuing Jesus. I feel my goals lie in God's work . . .His Word has inspired me so much that I want to tell everybody what He's done for me. . ."

Peeking into the future he notes, "the physical consequences of operating for Jesus in an area of conflict does little to hinder my desires. . .I want to do nothing that is opposite of God's will."

Later, on tour with the youth group, he is confronted with Isaiah 6, "Jesus kind of told me, 'This is for you!' Man, is it ever! I feel it is God asking me, 'Who will I send?' I am answering, 'I will go!' "

He continues, "My commitment to the work of Jesus may cost me my life. I am more than willing to pay the price! *'He who attempts to save his life will lose it, he who gives his life for My sake will keep it.'*"

* * * * *

While we were still living in Germany, Robert and I had a clash that needed discipline. So he was grounded for a few days. To make the time meaningful, I offered him Brother Andrew's book, "God's Smuggler," to read during his downtime. He was eleven or twelve at the time, and after reading it he expressed a great desire to meet someone who lived behind the Iron Curtain. Since we were living quite near the German east-west border, I suggested he pray; it would not be a difficult request for the Lord to answer.

Robert often asked his Dad to drive to that border where we could see the triple barbed wire fencing. We could watch the activity of border guards, and even get a glimpse of East

German farm families in the distance. This had a strong influence on Robert, especially seeing the little children at play and realizing the conflict and restrictions which overshadowed their lives.

About six years later in Oregon, we were hosting a home-group meeting. At one of these meetings, a member of our group brought a visitor from Yugoslavia. Robert was busy studying for school, but I immediately called him,

"Robert, someone is here you have been waiting to meet for a long time. Come and meet Mio!"

They met, and soon discovered that Mio spoke Slavic and German, while Robert spoke English and German. What a perfect match! Coincidence? Not at all! A Pastor in Yugoslavia, Mio could talk to our group which was so anxious to hear Mio's personal story. Robert was totally focused on this unexpected opportunity to do the English translation. We learned much about Mio's ministry behind the Iron Curtain, and the conditions surrounding the Christian community. Robert's excitement as he translated would be hard to describe!

It was obvious that a special bond was being formed: A God-planned friendship and an answered prayer! This was not a chance meeting, but a cherished gift. Robert's desire to go to Europe, Yugoslavia in particular, and see for himself and help in ministry was now not out of reach. He and Mio spent a lot of time talking about the possibilities once Robert's time at the Bible College was completed.

Now back to Robert's journal. . .

"Today is April 22, 1977. Today I didn't feel too good, but that's okay because Jesus really spoke to me nonetheless. First, on Monday I got a letter from Mio in Yugoslavia confirming Psalms 121 as a chapter from the Lord for me. The significance lies in the fact that the letter received was written on the eighth, which happens to be my birthday, and the same day Mom gave me the very same verses from the Lord."

Robert's journal includes this scripture that he received on his eighteenth birthday, April 8. 1977.

Psalm 121

I will lift up mine eyes unto the mountains, from whence cometh my help? My help comes from the Lord, Who made heaven and earth. He will not allow your foot to slip: He that keeps you will not slumber. Behold, He who keeps Israel will neither slumber nor sleep. The Lord is your keeper: The Lord is your shade on your right hand. The sun will not smite you by day, nor the moon by night. The Lord will protect you from all evil; He will keep your soul. The Lord will guard your going out and your coming in from this time forth, and forever.

"I feel that Jesus is trying to remind me of His protection and His promise to keep my foot from stumbling, which incidentally, is my nightmare. I'd rather die than lose my walk with Jesus. I love Jesus so much and I am to the point where I care about little else. Everything else seems so vain and useless. . .I've tried everything and everything is so tasteless after a while."

Then he explains: "I am sure that this is only one of the purging processes of Jesus so that all my love will be devoted to Him."

Then he writes about how important Bible reading had become; that it was passed being an occasional pursuit: "I really enjoy the Bible because it is so uplifting and encouraging. My life with Christ has become very peaceful. . .I have learned the secret of walking in faith. At all times we stand clean before Him when we are honest; then we can keep a cool relationship without hassle. So many times I've allowed a struggle to come between Jesus and me, for I would try to force myself to pray."

Then he compares himself to a flashlight, "yet without a battery there is no light to penetrate the darkness. I know that Christ has the key to the power that I need. How will I tap it? All seems so absurd! His Word is so peaceful, energizing, yet comforting. I can read it and be relaxed, yet I feel strength through my bones."

He stops his introspection for a prayer for help: "I love Jesus! Will You help me?! Please, Jesus, You are my only help. Give me hunger, thirst, quench me enough to keep me going. Help me to find the answers to my questions. Help me to continue to search for answers. Help me to find what I am searching for."

February 1978, he continues: "The calling of Christ is the beginning of His goals for my life in the sense that at that point His goals became my goals. In my youth, (he is only eighteen years old!) I was filled with an overwhelming curiosity that compelled me to discover the depth of subjects that were of interest to me. This interest could be either negative or positive, depending on how I would be walking with the Lord at the time. Probably since the Lord has really had control of my life, this strong urge toward that curiosity has been a strong positive force in my life and is the force that continues to bring me along even though I fail many times.

The first real interest that I had was in the area of geography and politics. Soon these interests became goals in my life for the future. However, it is to be noted that these were my goals, and God had little to do with them, as far as I was concerned.

After going back and forth in my spiritual life for a long time, I finally made a break for open ground, and my life with Christ began to take on a more solid shape. In other words, I finally struck (like a gold-miner) with something. From this point on, my goals were His goals and His goals were my goals.

My goals became transformed to the point that I actually desired God's will for my life. The problem, that usually arises in this situation, is that one will inadvertently mistake God's will for one's own will. This happened to me, but God knew that I was really going for it, so He allowed this to continue in order to eventually purge my desires. Then for a time, I really didn't know what my desires were. This was an especially strange time for me because I felt as if I were exiled or something of that nature. I really didn't know where I was going until God waited for me to pull that hidden desire deep out of my heart; the desire to be involved in God's ministry.

Probably the greatest desire of my life now that I am trying to follow Christ, is to really be of help to people. To really have a place in the lives of people by knowing that I have something to offer. This is what I desire. I don't feel this is selfish at all. Matter of fact, I know it's not selfish, because I want to give of myself."

* * * * *

Jesus, My Friend

Jesus, Jesus, You're my Friend,
I will love You to the end.
You have taken all my desire,
Cleansed all with Your perfect fire.
There have been so many fears,
So many stinging tears.
But as I seek Your glowing grace
The tears are washed from my face.

You became as an oppressed Man,

Pressed under a ruthless hand,
To take from me all my chains
And free me from him who feigns.
Hah! Where is that yoke that held me bound?
It's gone, since You I've found!

The mysteries I sought, the passions I fought,
All fruitless endeavors You have brought to naught.

Jesus You are the Path of Life,
A path that leads through all strife,
The fire may sting, but will not burn-
Those who don't make it, how can I mourn?
The door is open for all to go through,
Many reject it, even though it's true.
-Robert Reid Muthmann

*   *   *   *   *

We are like clay in the Potter's hands. . .

Turning
   Turning
      Pinching
         Rolling
Molding
   Squeezing
      Pushing
         Pulling

All with gentle hands He's shaping,
Working daily with the clay,
Till He sees His dear Son's image
In that vessel made of clay!

But You, O Lord, You are our Father, we are the clay, and You are the Potter, and all we are the work of Your hand. (Isaiah 64:8)

For it is God who is at work in you both to will and to do for His good pleasure. (Philippians 2:13)

For whom He foreknew, He also predestined to become conformed to the image of His Son. (Romans 8:29)

*   *   *   *   *

The process Robert went through finally brought him to the peaceful realization that God's will could become his will, God's goals could be his goals, and God's desires his desires. Through the struggles, God gives the impulse to yield, the desire for His good pleasure to be the goal of our working and doing. As parents it had been astonishing to see how rapidly God was working in Robert's life. After these last words of his journal it was only about six months until Jesus called him Home. We see our heavenly Father behind every struggle, His continued love and guidance through every stretch and failure until His desires were accomplished. It is just recently we learned that Robert's life is still ministering to people who knew him, and even the next generation who never met him. Doing His will and His desires comes slowly, too. God knows how and at what speed to bring His completion to our place in the Kingdom. His will in each life is specific and important to Him.

At this point for Jay and me, God's will in our family situation is our will. Together we are doing what God asks for our daughter for this particular time. Changes will come, for that we wait on Him. Our son has been given to Jesus over and over again. Grief has its own way of returning, by memories, by seeing or hearing from his friends, and many other ways. If grief has visited you (and whom has it not visited?) you know what I am talking about. It is not uncommon for one of us to say, "I just now felt that Robert was here!" Now he is one of the great "cloud of witnesses" (Hebrews 12:1).

What do any of us know about this wonderful gift of children? The life of each does not stretch out in a straight forward path. As parents we can say, our life raising our children has been composed of decades of training, learning, and praying for strength and wisdom. But what we see is a beautiful life unfolding before us; not just for Robert, but also for Shiona's life. It was a profound question she asked before she was four years old.

We were on the way home from a visit with family friends when she suddenly asked, "Why am I here, why am I alive?" How do you put the answer in a way such a young child could grasp? I can't remember exactly how we answered, but certainly something about Jesus. We were stunned, but we kept the words simple. It was a question to go back to many times. She was at this time singing about Jesus, for Jesus, and to Jesus day after day. I can still see her sitting on the top bunk, singing as though she were in the choir loft with Jesus as her audience!

Now she knows and is sincerely confident in what Jesus has given her to do. He has only expanded on what she has been doing all her life. She prays after each encounter, whether it is someone who seems not interested, someone who needs encouragement or a person of mutual under-standing of faith in Jesus. We step back and watch the mar-velous work that God has done in her and for her. We can honestly say, "This is the Lord's doing, it is marvelous in our eyes." It's true the difficulties, grieving times, the hardships, and all the answers are not given, but we can look to Jesus, the Author and Finisher of our faith. We can look forward with anticipation, and we can look back and see His plan. Right now we can keep looking up in daily expectation for another adventure with Jesus.

Living and working under our Master Builder requires focus. His plan is in our hands; which is His Word. Listening for Him to speak to us, and then obeying is our responsibility. God requires us to come and to wait for Him. All we like sheep, don't always find this easy. We don't enjoy being agitated when obstructions come in the way of "onward-forward." Is our focus temporarily eroding? Maybe so, since we are ever learning, each obstacle is a new or repeat lesson or refinement. Then we go back to being still, letting be, and knowing that He is God (Psalm 46:10). There is a poem of John Oxenham which I often repeat to myself. You may be familiar with it:

> *With thoughtless and impatient hands,*
> *We tangle up the plans the Lord hath wrought,*
> *And when we cry in pain, He saith,*
> *"Be quiet, dear, while I untie the knot."*

This gentle admonition brings back my focus. It is a reminder that God *is* in control. It is time again to heed the lesson to follow on with the Master Builder, who knows our desire to build according to His plan and specifications.

All Your works shall praise You, O Lord, and Your loving ones shall bless You. (Psalm 145:10 AMP)

Chapter Seventeen

The Upward Look

Noah's Project

The Lord sat as King at the flood, the Lord sits as King forever. (Psalm 29:10)

In reading the story of Noah, I have found that Psalm 34 is a good accompaniment to the narrative. We know that King David was not there in Noah's time, but God has dealt with His people and His creation with constancy of purpose all through His Word. We can take a peek at David's psalm along with the account of Noah and perhaps find it useful. You will discover Psalm 34 interspersed as you read on.

God designed a dwelling for Noah. God assigned work for him to do. One day Noah called his wife and family and showed them the Floating Fortress they were to live in, a Favored Place, and a Secret Place. It was their Ark of Safety. Then the animals came, some two by two, and some by sevens. God designed it all. (Noah's story begins in Genesis 6).

God invited them to come into the Ark. There they were safe, leaving all the chaos and violence behind. Likewise, Jesus invites us to abide with Him; to come aside to the place where His Presence dwells, away from the hurry, the rush, and disturbances that cry out to penetrate our quiet.

Taste and see that the Lord is good; blessed is the man who takes refuge in Him. Fear the Lord, you His saints, for those who fear Him (like Noah and family) *lack nothing.* (Psalm 34:9)

God prepares a way of escape and makes provision. When we go to Him and ask, He will shut the door to the worries and pressures of our day. Noah was a righteous man.

The righteous cry out, the Lord hears them; the Lord is close to the brokenhearted and saves those who are crushed in spirit. A righteous man may have many troubles, but the Lord delivers him from them all. The foes of the righteous (an entire civilization in Noah's time) *will be condemned. The Lord redeems His servants; no one will be condemned who takes refuge in Him.* (Psalm 34:17-19, 21-22).

These few verses certainly describe Noah's time and his personal reaction to what was happening in his day and time. His cry out to the Lord was answered with a Plan. His desire then is also for us to look to Him, listen, and obey as did Noah and his family. When God told Noah it was time for them to enter the Ark, He was putting them in a place which disallowed them to be saddened and disquieted by the sudden desperate clamor for life, and the burial of the violence that grieved Noah, and more so, the Almighty.

Could it be that sometimes God has to shut us away so that He can do the work He needs to do, without our interference, all the while keeping us in His love, surrounded with His compassion and care? As illustrated in Noah's story, we should never think we are outside of His will. We are His beloved ones. Listen to the quiet hush in the Ark of Safety when God shut the door and they realized what all this meant. Many are the times God has provided protection and a hiding place for His people through the ages, generation after generation.

I sought the Lord, and He answered me; He delivered me from all my fears. Those who look to Him are radiant; their faces are never covered with shame. This poor man called, and the Lord heard him; He saved him out of all his troubles. (Psalm 34:4-6)

Looking up to Jesus and our Father is a good lesson to learn as we read about the specifications of the Ark given to Noah directly from God. We know there was a window or opening either in the roof, near the roof, or around the roof. (Depending on which translation you have in your hand.) Wherever your mind places this opening, let it be a reminder of an upward look; just as the upward look was necessary for Noah and family. They couldn't look anywhere else, only up. Thinking of Noah's window should help encourage us to direct our focus away from the culture that greedily tries to eat us up. "Looking unto Jesus the Author and Finisher of our faith" is the message found in Hebrews 12:2.

Picture Noah guiding the family on a tour through this temporary home. At first they must have felt very closed-in. Were the Ark-dwellers surprised that rain was not pelting in on them? Gathering around, looking up, rain falling, but not coming into the Ark, may have been a question. They must have been amazed! We would like to ask, "Was there only one window? How big was the window? What was keeping the rain out?" They did not have the Word of God to read for themselves about the protection of angel wings. But we read many times about that protection in the Word. That the Ark was accompanied by angels should not be beyond belief.

The angel of the Lord encamps around those who fear Him, and He delivers them. (Psalm 34:7)

Can't you envision angel wings covering and protecting the window (or windows) just as God designed the cherubim to cover another Ark, the Ark of the Covenant? Could it be that angel wings were the "transparent material unknown to us" as one Bible commentary says about the window? Whether the window was in the roof or surrounding the roof, we know rain was coming down, but not coming into and flooding the Ark. I like the idea of angel wings covering and protecting the Ark just as God promises that angel wings are protecting His people.

He will cover you with His pinions, and under His wings shall you trust and find refuge. For He will give His angels (especial) charge over you, to accompany and defend and preserve you in all your ways (of obedience and service). (Psalm 91:4, 11 AMP)

What a wonderful promise to hide in our hearts! One of God's constant promises for all of His people, then and now! Of course, God had special purposes for His building specification. We shouldn't wonder that God wanted them to have light, air, and water; all in the correct measurements in order to bring needed refreshment to the inhabitants living under His protection. Likewise, He wants us to have Light, Breath and Water; all found in our Lord Jesus Christ, who, I believe, was right there with them. Before you disagree with me, please remember that Jesus walked in the fiery furnace with three Hebrew boys, and with Daniel in the lion's den.

He says in Isaiah 43:2-3, "When you pass through the waters, I will be with you; and through the rivers, they will not overflow you. When you walk through the fire, you will not be scorched, nor will the flame burn you."

For I am the Lord your God. And, the Lord sits as King forever. (Psalm 29:10)

Past, present, and future! Jesus Christ is the same yesterday and today, yes, and forever! (Hebrews 13:8).

There must have been a lot of conversation that day. Why? What? Where? When? How? Noah would be the best preacher and teacher for this day of days. His heart must have been full as he talked to his family! 2 Peter 2:5 tells that Noah was a preacher of righteousness. Maybe he said some things like this:

Come, my children, listen to me; I will teach you the fear of the Lord. Whoever of you loves life and desires to see many good days, keep your tongue from evil and your lips from speaking lies. Turn from evil and do good; seek peace and pursue it. The eyes of the Lord are on the righteous and His ears are attentive to their cry; the face of the Lord is against those who do evil, to cut off the memory of them from the earth. (Psalm 34:11-16)

Perhaps Noah said, "We need to talk to God. We need to keep looking up; up to God who is our Savior from this flood. He is our Protector. He is in Heaven, He is also with us. We will talk to God right now, and thank Him for His provision for our safety and for the safety of the animals. Come, join hands, we'll sing praises to God our Father, who has graciously provided for us."

I will extol the Lord at all times; His praise will always be on my lips. My soul will boast in the Lord; let the afflicted hear and rejoice. Glorify the Lord with me; let us exalt His name together. (Psalm 34:1-3)

"He is protecting us. God gave the plan, told me the measurements, and told me what wood to use. He has been an encouragement to me all these many, many years. It was a lot of work, you all helped in many ways, but God also gave the strength to do it. All our trust must be in Him. Without Him it would never have been possible. His Name be praised. Now let's get to work. There are many animals to feed. Sounds like some of them are hungry already!"

There are a number of significant characteristics about Noah that should attract our attention.

- He reverenced God, putting his trust wholly in Him.
- He didn't have any written Word, but he believed when God talked to him.
- When given a monumental task, he obeyed and toiled far beyond anyone else we could read about in the Bible.
- He endured persecution as he delivered the Words God gave him warning rebellious people who mocked and scorned him.

Then came that wonderful day when Noah sent out the dove for the second time. In awe, he received the dove back when it brought him an olive leaf. Life! Life had come back to them! Noah and family now knew that God remembered them and life was given again to the creation He had made. What gladness must have accompanied them as they left the Ark! Then Noah built an altar and together they worshiped the Lord who sat as King at the flood. God honors those who honor Him. Noah was honored when God made the covenant with him that the earth would never again be destroyed by water. The glorious rainbow is the token of that covenant!

Our God has a plan for us, a good plan to give us a future and a hope (Jeremiah 29:11).

The Word also says, "He who began a good work in you
will perfect it until the day of Christ Jesus" (Philippians 1:6).
It may take a while to absorb all that He is asking of us, just
as in Noah's life. Jesus is the Provision God has given us.
Jesus is our Ark of Safety. We can take our eyes away from
the evil around us and know His presence daily, even hourly
or better, moment by moment. He will not leave us helpless.
He will not leave us without the material to build with and
accomplish the task. Like Noah, "we are His workmanship,
created in Christ Jesus for good works, which God prepared
beforehand, that we should walk in them" (Ephesians 2:10).
There will be the testing times when it seems He is saying:

*"Will you trust Me? Will you wait for Me? Will you lean
on Me? Keep looking up. And when you are tired or discouraged I will not scold you. I will sustain you and even
when everything seems dark around you, I will show you
treasures of darkness, and the hidden wealth of secret
places, so that you will know that it is I, the Lord, the
God of Israel, who calls you by your name."* (Proverbs
3:5; Psalm 27:14; Song of Solomon 8:5; Psalm 103:12,
145:14; Isaiah 45:3)

*   *   *   *   *

Reach for Joy

Some time ago feeling frustrated and losing motivation,
I prayed and the words that came were, "Help me. . .reach
for joy!" I hadn't thought out the words "reach for joy" and
I was a little startled repeating them over and over, "Reach
for joy! If you need joy, reach for it." It hit the right cord
with me. Thinking about it, I realized it was the Holy Spirit
teaching me something. It was something I needed for those
times when concerns get out of control, when perspective

gets lost in the rubble and the trouble, even though I know God can answer any request.

What I find myself doing is trying to plow through on my own, which serves only to increase the pressure and make the situation muddier. If we need joy, patience, strength, kindness and love, all we need to do is reach for it. He was reminding me in a new way.

Then my thoughts and fingers went to John 20:27-28, a passage where I remembered Jesus using the word "reach." I wanted to read this in the Word. It is the well-known story about Jesus appearing to His disciples and one was missing. When Thomas was told about Jesus rising again, he was quite unbelieving, saying, "Unless I see Him and touch His hands and His side, I will not believe." It wasn't long until the next time Jesus appeared, and there with the others was Thomas. He didn't have to say a word. Jesus already knew that he was troubled with doubts and simply said, "Reach out your hand. . .don't be doubting and unbelieving." Thomas, with faith, reached out and believed: "My Lord and my God." Instant recognition and belief!

Isn't it wonderful that Jesus knows our needs even before we ask? He does not upbraid us even if we have doubts. He is ready to respond with a word, "Reach!" and we have the filling for strength, patience, endurance or whatever is our need. Jesus is here in every kind of nearness. He is ready with every kind of readiness. All we need to do is reach. He takes us immediately as we are and teaches us so patiently, and even unexpectedly.

It is calming, even thrilling to read, He came to His disciples and said, "Peace be unto you!" (John 20:19). He gives it so readily and offers it freely, blessing upon blessing and grace for grace. "Freely you have received, freely give" (Matthew 10:8). Never does He say, "Oh, short supply, come back later."

Thinking about this, reminds me of stories Jay tells about living in short supply, especially for bread, during the war years in Germany. Many times he stood, instead of his mother, in a long line for bread. Then getting right up to the moment of having a loaf in his hand, the clerk would say, "Sorry, no more bread, come back tomorrow!" He took his empty hands and stomach back home. That never happens when we go to Jesus. He is always ready, always has more to give; even exceeding abundantly above all that we ask or think (Ephesians 3:20). So when feeling depleted, or an emergency confronts, I will reach and He will give. Help is always beyond and above; beyond ourselves reaching to Jesus, above ourselves to see again from His perspective. It's as simple as renewing our focus.

It was just after a hospital stay. Shiona was home and frustrated again in trying to regain her confidence in grooming, especially doing her hair. As women we know how particular we are, not just about hair, but all grooming. I could hear, though, what Shiona was going through and, at the next doctor visit that was one of the topics.

"When will I ever be able to do the things I want to do so badly?"

There was not much help from the doctor; men just don't always get it when it comes to these feminine desires.

During one of these morning frustrations, I heard singing from the bathroom. "Oh, this is going better today," I thought.

Then I heard an urgent request, "Mom, get your pencil and write this down. Quick, get the music down, too. Please."

The following is the song that was born that morning. Right then came release from the frustration. The Helper was there. We still sing this song often. It fits so many anxious moments, and calls us back to the Snoopy reminder, "Keep looking up, it's the only way to live!"

Keep your focus on the Lord,
Keep your focus on the Lord,
We will never get discouraged,
We will sing unto the Lord.

Never, never get discouraged,
For the Lord, our God, is King.
Thank Him now for all His goodness;
Jesus Christ is always there.

Keep your focus on the Lord,
We will never more lose hope.
We will nevermore be fearful,
We will always praise the Lord.
-Shiona Ann Muthmann

Thanks be to God, who always leads us in His triumph in
Christ, and manifests through us the sweet aroma of the
knowledge of Him in every place. (2 Corinthians 2:14)

O LORD
OUR LORD

HOW MAJESTIC
IS THY NAME

IN ALL
THE EARTH

Ps 8:1

Chapter Eighteen

Behold Your God

The Autographed Life

Heavenly Father,
My life has been written by Your own Hand. You are
the Author of my life. This is too exalted for me and causes
me to greatly reverence Your Name. You have autographed
my life with Your indelible pen. I belong to You. You love
me with Your immeasurable love. I live within that love.
This is too great for my human mind to grasp. I bow in
thankfulness to You.

Preserve and sustain Your Word in my life as You have
preserved and sustained Your written Word through all the
ages from the beginning even until now. Through wars, famines, plagues, hate, evil, torture, and every kind of onslaught
from the enemy Your Word has prevailed.

You are the Great Sustainer, Provider, and Life-giver.
Keep me, hold me, and draw me ever closer to You, that I
may see more and more clearly Your ways, Your workings,
and learn more of Your wisdom, Your grace, Your love, and
Your patience. Bring to life Your Word in my life.

I thank and praise Your Holy Name today through Your
Dear Son, Jesus Christ, my Lord and Savior. Help me to
be diligent to hold fast, to draw near, to press on, and even

when weary, yet always pursuing; and more so; caught and sustained in Your Love.

My love and my whole life I give to You, my Father

Out of the Ivory Palaces
He Came to Bring Me. . .

Out of my darkness . . . into His light. (Isaiah 60:1)
Out of my depths . . . . . into His nearness.(Jeremiah 23:23)
Out of my furnace . . . . into His glory. (Isaiah 43:2)
Out of my cave. . . . . . . into His home. (Psalm 68:6)
Out of my prison . . . . . into His freedom. (Isaiah 61:1)
Out of my wilderness . . into His grace. (Isaiah 41:18-19)
Out of my weariness . . into His strength. (Isaiah 40:11)
Out of my valley . . . . . into His spring. (Psalm 84:6)
Out of my shame . . . . . into His joy. (Isaiah 61:7)
Out of my loneliness . . into His love. (Jeremiah 31:3)
Out of my danger . . . . . into His safety. (Psalm 12:5)
Out of my poverty . . . . into His wealth.(Philippians 4:19)

Blessed by the Lord, who daily bears our burden, the God who is our Salvation. (Psalm 68:20)

How Majestic Is Thy Name

How do we describe majesty? Use a dictionary? Look at human royalty? Do we list the trappings of the throne room in any country ruled by royalty or dictator and be more than satisfied—even wanting to stay there? What do we see when we look at copies of *real* Majesty? Disappointment? It doesn't take long for the glittering gold, the diamonds, emeralds, sapphires, and rubies to fascinate us greater than the mere human form so elegantly clothed and garnished. King David, in Psalm 8, calls out: "How majestic is Thy Name in all the earth." This is the greatest king Israel ever had talking about the King of kings and Lord of lords. In 1 Samuel 2:30, our King says, "Those who honor Me I will honor, and those who despise Me will be lightly esteemed." Now, how to honor His Majestic Name? Psalm 50:15, 23 says, "Call upon Me in the day of trouble; I shall rescue you, and you will honor Me. He who offers a sacrifice of thanksgiving honors Me; and to him who orders his way aright I shall show the salvation of God." So here we see clearly where we fit and where God stands. In Micah 6:8, "He has told you, O man, what is good; and what does the Lord require of you, but to do justice, to love kindness and to walk humbly with your God."

A peek into the Bible and we see rather quickly that we are not at the top deserving honor, exaltation, and adoration. We see One who is all deserving, all wise. Isaiah 9:6 foretells, "For a child will be born to us, a son will be given to us; and the government will rest on His shoulders; and His name will be called Wonderful Counselor, Mighty God, Eternal Father, Prince of Peace." Then we bow to Him in our need and Jesus washes us clean in His blood; that scarlet thread that runs all through Scripture from Genesis all the way to Revelation. "There is no other way, no other name under heaven whereby we can be saved" (Acts 4:12), and enter into a relationship with Him; knowing Him, the only One who is above all-all kings, authorities, dictators and despots; benevolent or cruel.

This God is our majestic God. He does amazing things. There is a very interesting story in Judges 13 about a man and his wife who had no children. That was a hard thing to bear for Israelites. Then one day Manoah's wife was visited by the Angel of the Lord. He told her that she would conceive and give birth to a son. She told her husband about this visit. After Manoah prayed, the Angel of the Lord appeared a second time. In the course of this visit, Manoah asked the name of their Visitor. He answered, "Why do you ask, seeing it is secret?" (v.18). Why a secret Name? Does God keep secrets? I think so.

Deuteronomy 29:29 tells us "secret things belong to the Lord." Manoah and his wife were very frightened when they prepared an offering, and this Visitor went up in the flame of the fire that consumed the offering. When Manoah and his wife saw this, they fell on their faces to the ground (V. 18). They knew they had a Majestic Visitor. Has your life been met by the Majestic Visitor? Now we ask, too. What was that secret Name? At His birth they were told for the very first time, "Call His name Jesus, for it is He who will save His people from their sins" (Matthew 1:21). A Secret, a Majestic Secret, safely kept from before the foundation of the world; certainly something to ponder and wonder over.

Our lives also are secrets that have been safely kept. Did you ever wonder about that? Go back and read Psalm 139 again. It says, to everyone who reads it, that we were made in secret. You were a secret. The beginning of all life is a secret. God only, the Majestic God, knew all about you before your parents knew you. Do you really want any other King over your life? This Psalm also tells us that He understands us better than we understand ourselves, that He is intimately acquainted with our ways, and that He has laid His hand upon us. How can we not say with King David, "Lead me in the everlasting way" (v.24)? I don't want any other way than His way; how about you?

Any other ruler, king or governor is not out from under the King of kings and Lord of lords. Who else can call us clean when we bow before Him at His feet? So let's see How Majestic is His Name works out right here and now, in everyday life, even very difficult life. The 1930's were very turbulent years in many parts of the world (sounds like the times we are living in today!) Jay and his brother were born and grew up during the Hitler dictatorship in Germany. Their father was the pastor of an evangelical church, precisely known as the Confessing Church, which took a strong stand against Hitler, the despicable despot who entertained delusions of ruling the world. Jay's mother, Lilli, was her husband's helper in the congregation, teaching the women and children in weekly classes. They knew that everything about their church was under surveillance by the Gestapo, so they lived and taught circumspectly under God's guidance. However the day came when Lilli was ordered to report to the authorities. She went and appeared before the group of uniformed officials by herself—at least that's what the officers thought. They thought that she was caught and alone like in the spider's web! Then the questions began.

"What do you do to help the effort?"

"God has given me work to do!" came her strong, clear, and distinct answer.

"What might that be?" was the next scornful question.

"I have my children to raise and my husband to help in his work."

Was she scared? I'm sure she was, but God says, those who honor Me, I will honor.

Abruptly, one officer turned to the others saying, "We don't need her kind here. Get rid of her!"

Get rid of her? What would that mean? Surely, a very difficult message to hear! Did her heart pound? Of course, it did! What will happen next? Yes, it did happen that pastors and Christians as well as Jews, were sent to concentration camps. Their stories are awesome and noteworthy, and the outcomes many times, horrific. But for Lilli, at this very moment, His Majesty spoke, not audibly. But He spoke! These officers were summarily over-ruled. They sent her HOME! Yes, they sent her back to her husband, her children, and church family! Our God reigns! Lilli loved to sing, and this Psalm may be what she sang with all her heart that day:

Thou art my God and I will praise Thee, Thou art my God I will exalt Thee. Oh give thanks unto the Lord, for He is good, and His mercy endureth forever! (Psalm 118:28-29 KJV)

Yes, they sent her home. A miracle! She trained her children in God's ways and continued teaching the women, meeting them at night, as they quietly walked in the dark to the manse to hear God's Word and learn to honor, obey, and give thanks for all things. The village children came for playtime with the pastor's wife, where they learned the stories of the Old Testament and of Jesus, the Savior, in the New Testament. They heard how God's people overcame, were courageous, saw miracles, and trusted Jehovah. Lilli and Erich Muthmann, faithful witnesses and workers in God's Kingdom, served and honored Him through a most difficult era in German history.

Thank You, Dearest Father, for faithful and courageous witnesses through whom You have displayed Your Majesty.

Where before us or in the history books is there a king, a ruler, or leader like our God? There is none! In Isaiah 40 there are some interesting questions God speaks to us.

To whom then will you liken God? Or what likeness will you compare with Him? Do you not know? Have you not heard? He it is who reduces rulers to nothing, who makes the judges of the earth meaningless. He merely blows on them, and they wither and the storm carries them away like stubble. To whom then will you liken Me that I should be his equal? (Isaiah 40:18, 21, 23-25)

We can fully trust our God no matter what the future holds. Times may get darker, but now we can day by day prepare ourselves and our families with the Word of God. We have the opportunity now to seek the Lord with all our hearts so that the Holy Spirit can use the equipment we've stored away for the trials that may lie ahead. We want to get it down deep in our spirits, so that we are abiding in Him. Reading and rereading Jesus' teachings to His disciples makes strong our foundation. Jesus Christ is the Vine. The branches will bear fruit if they abide in the Vine; without Him we can do nothing (see John 15:5). There are two verses in Malachi 3:16-17 that have encouraged Jay and me along with close friends.

Then those who feared the Lord spoke often to one another, and the Lord gave attention and heard it, and a book of remembrance was written before Him for those who fear the Lord and who esteem His name. "And they will be Mine," says the Lord of hosts, "on the day that I prepare My own possession, and I will spare them as a Man spares his own son who serves him."

Jay and I want to be in that book of remembrance of His, and we want to be there with our families and dear friends that the Lord has given us. We want you to be there, too! Majestic is His Name Who calls us Friends—His own possession. What privileged people we are! There is no other King and no other Kingdom!

God is to us a God of deliverances; and to God the Lord belong escapes from death. (Psalm 68:20)

* * * * *

Majestic Servant-King

Not for Himself. . .
The Savior came to walk the dusty roads.
Not for Himself. . .
To learn the carpenter's shop, even servant hood.
Not for himself. . .

Water to wine, thousands to feed.
Not for himself...
To quench His thirst, only Living Water to give.
Not for Himself...
As a joyful widow receives her son.
Not for Himself...
His robe to touch, the blind to see, ten lepers cleansed.
Not for Himself...
O'er Jerusalem to weep, scorn to endure.

Not for Himself...
The upper room, the bread, the cup. Betrayed!
Not for Himself...
Great drops of blood, the bitterest cup to drink.
Not for Himself...
To hang on the tree, to rise again.
But for Himself...
The spotless Bride, eternally!

Hallelujah! For the Lord our God, the Almighty, reigns. Let us rejoice and be glad and give the glory unto Him, for the marriage of the Lamb has come and His bride has made herself ready. Blessed are those who are invited to the marriage supper of the Lamb. (Revelation 19:6-7, 9)

* * * * *

Knowing His Name

Thankful for the day that we first opened our hearts to the Lord Jesus Christ, we begin to wonder, "How do I get to know Him better!" Just as you do about anyone you first meet, the natural desire is to spend time with your new friend, as much time as possible. So it is with our new Friend, Jesus. He gave us His Book; actually it is a love letter. It is personal and it is necessary for growth in our new life. His love is the first taste, "For God so loved. . .He gave His Son" (John 3:16). We read the gospels, especially John, because in that book we hear more than in any other place what Jesus had to say and teach His disciples. In John's book we learn some essentials that tell us plainly about Jesus' character. We find out in His words, "I am the Bread of Life; I am the Light of the world; I am the Door" (John 6:35; 9:5; 10:7). Read on and we find further unfolding of Who Jesus is.

Then in learning more about Him, we discover, (usually with the help of a Bible teacher) that there are Compound Redemptive Names of Jehovah, which mean, "I am what I am, or I will be Who I will be" (Exodus 3:14-16). Referring back to college days and using the textbook of Dean K. J. Connor, I have copied the following. I am not suggesting a deep study, but just a look at what His Name means which is helpful and comforting. The Majestic Name of our God cannot be spoken in a sentence, so use this outline to acquaint yourself with the Person to whom you've committed your life.

Jehovah Elohim	Genesis 2:4	The Lord, our Creator
Jehovah El Elyon	Genesis 14:22	The Lord, the Most High God, the Owner
Jehovah Adonia	Genesis 15:2	The Lord, the Master
Jehovah El Olam	Genesis 21:33	The Lord, the Everlasting
Jehovah Jireh	Genesis 22:14	The Lord, the Provider

Jehovah Rapha	Exodus 15:26	The Lord, the Healer
Jehovah Nissi	Exodus 17:15	The Lord, the Banner
Jehovah Makaddesh	Exodus 31:13	The Lord, our Sanctification
Jehovah Shalom	Judges 6:24	The Lord, our Peace
Jehovah Shaphat	Judges 11:27	The Lord, the Judge
Jehovah Saboath	1 Samuel 1:3	The Lord of Hosts
Jehovah Zidkenu	Jeremiah 23:6	The Lord, our Righteousness
Jehovah Raah	Psalm 23:1	The Lord the Shepherd
Jehovah Elyon	Psalm 7:17	The Lord, the Blesser
Jehovah Hosenu	Psalm 95:6	The Lord, the Maker
Jehovah Gibbor	Isaiah 42:13	The Lord, the Mighty
Jah-Jehovah	Isaiah 12:2, 26:4	The Lord, the Jehovah
Jehovah Shammah	Ezekiel 48:35	The Lord, the Everpresent
Jehovah Jehoshua Messiah	Matthew 1:21, Acts 2:36	The Lord Jesus Christ

Each of these Names, relative to our needs, finds its ultimate fulfillment in the greatest Compound Redemptive Name ever revealed, and as unfolded in the New Testament; this Name is the **Lord Jesus Christ**. It is divinely suitable that the Redemptive Names of God find their consummation in the Redeemer Himself. (Quoting from Kevin Connor. Thank you!).

I find this tabulation of Compound Redemptive Names of Jehovah a comforting list to refer to in times of need. It is all encompassing, and certainly gives support to the words beginning and ending Psalm 8, "O lord, our Lord, how Majestic is Thy Name in all the earth." And in Song of Solomon 1:3, "Thy Name is as ointment poured forth." These Words help us in realizing what Treasure we have in this God in whom we have come to trust. "For this God is our God forever and ever; He will be our guide even to the end" (Psalm 48:14).

Throughout our lives we keep learning about this Name. Probably one of the earliest we learn is Savior, and then we learn He is also called the Healer, the Provider, and more as we encounter obstacles and trials. We keep finding the resource we need in that Name, whether we travel the wilderness, a rough road or a path with sharp turns ahead. He is there—the God who is Ever Present, who Cares, the One who is lavish in His Caring. Since all of the above have been poured out in His Love-Sacrifice for all, how can we not say with the Bride in Song of Solomon 5:16, "He is altogether lovely. This is my Beloved and this is my Friend!"

*   *   *   *   *

This is one of the last paintings of Robert's. It was painted on his bedroom wall as a mural. Of course we don't have the wall anymore, but this photograph we treasure. It reflects and reminds how we find true Life and true Light, if we want to be sure of our eternal destiny. It illustrates Jesus' own Words from Matthew 7:13-14.

> *Enter through the narrow gate. For wide is the gate and broad is the road that leads to destruction, and many enter through it. But small is the gate and narrow the road that leads to life, and only a few find it.*

In the painting Jesus is represented by the sun and tree, as the Son of Righteousness and the Tree of Life. The nations (culture and world) and danger of destruction are represented by the sea and rocks in the foreground. Here are Robert's comments on this picture: "Tonight I saw a road that forked. One was two lanes and the other was one lane and narrow. It was dry country and the wide road seemed to be the obvious

308

road to take, but leads to eternal sorrow; take the narrow road, because on that road you will reach the destination of everlasting joy!"

The prayer of Robert and our family is that if you are reading this and have not entered the narrow gate that Jesus tells of, please stop now and give your heart and life to Jesus. He made the way possible for all and He is lovingly calling you to come.

*   *   *   *

Living Beyond the Fringes

A woman comes to Jesus begging for healing for her daughter. Jesus identifies her as a Gentile, and declares His coming is for the Jews. She acknowledges that she is alien to the house of Israel, nevertheless she has a monumental problem: Her daughter is demon possessed. Where else can she go? Is there another god that is His equal? In her extreme need she has come to the only One who can heal her darling. So she presses Him all the more, asking only for a crumb from the children's bread. In effect she is acknowledging her place, her humble place, but she is *reaching to touch the fringe* and asking for the least bit: just a crumb.

"Yes, Lord, I am a Gentile, I am not worthy, but just a crumb will be enough."

Jesus responds, "O woman, your faith is great; be it done for you as you wish."

And her daughter was healed at once. (Matthew 15:27)

Remember Ruth. She was not of Israel, and desired only the fragments left behind by the reapers. Yet she was blessed abundantly. Before she really knew who Boaz was, he blessed her saying, "May the Lord reward your work, and your wages be full from the Lord, the God of Israel, under whose wings you have come to seek refuge" (Ruth 2:12).

She was no longer on the outside looking in. She was beginning to move passed the fringes.

Then there was a man born blind in order that the works of God might be displayed in him (John 9). Very soon after his healing he became a significant agitation to the Pharisees. Without realizing it, he was pointing out their blindness which was spiritual. "You fellows don't see. Did you ever heal a blind man or hear of such a thing? You can see, that's wonderful, but there's more to sight and *that you can't see!* This man must be from God!" They put him out of the synagogue. Then Jesus came to the one He healed, and declared himself as the Son of Man, and immediately our friend confessed, "Lord, I believe," and he worshiped Him.

In the next chapter we learn about the Good Shepherd, and how He loves and cares for His sheep. "The sheep hear His voice, and He calls His own sheep by name, and He leads them out" (John 10:1-3). Even though the man was healed and then cast out by the authorities, he was actually led out by the True Shepherd. By being led out, he was being brought in beyond the fringes!

O, dear Jesus, carpenter of Nazareth, Who builds our lives; may our lives be showcases that display Your mercy, goodness, and loving-kindness. May we also join with many who with heart, soul, and mind have given praise, honor and glory to Your Precious Name.

Can you recall to mind Mephibosheth? He's a long-time favorite of mine, and was a "least of" in the house of king Saul, lame and lonely—yet called out by King David. For what purpose?

That I may show him kindness for Jonathan's sake. . .and David said to him, "Do not fear, for I will surely show kindness to you for the sake of your father Jonathan, and will restore to you all the land of your grandfather

Saul; and you shall eat at my table continually."....So Mephibosheth ate at David's table as one of the king's sons. (2 Samuel 9:1, 7, 11)

He became another one brought in beyond the fringe. It was no longer just a longing. Now he was near enough to learn who David was, this close friend and confidant of his father. Besides that he was seated at the table with the royal family. Promises and privileges for Mephi!

He brought me to the banqueting table, His banner over me is love. (Song of Solomon 2:4)

Jesus is calling for you and for me: "Behold I stand at the door and knock; if anyone hears My voice and opens the door, I will come in to him, and will dine with him, and he with Me" (Revelation 3:20). What a grand invitation! To sit with Him at His table! If you haven't done so yet, come close and touch the fringes of His ways. When you first come, it is a growing time. Soon you realize more and more how much and how boundless is His love for you. Then (hopefully) you begin writing things down; things He has whispered to you, or showed you as you read His Word; memories that will encourage you toward thankfulness, and in loving and trusting Him even in the midst of trial. These tokens of love, like seeds, will grow tall as you recollect them from time to time.

Softly and tenderly Jesus is calling,
Calling for you and for me;
See, on the portals He's waiting and watching,
Watching for you and for me.
-W. L. Thompson

*   *   *   *   *

We had been in Germany about two and a half years, when we felt the urgent need to return to the States. It was about the time that Shiona had the fall causing her head injury.

Jay was the first to feel this urging, so we began praying together earnestly for the Lord's direction. From time to time I had been reading the autobiography of George Mueller (founder of orphanages in Bristol, England during the nineteenth century). His habit of praying for daily needs, needs far beyond what ours were at the time, impressed us. We would read parts of his story, glean a little, and pray more.

Jay's decision to leave the company would put us on our own—travel plans and financing would be up to us—since it was our choice. The company was sorry to see us leave, and we knew it would be a big undertaking. As we continued to pray we made a list of the costs and the finances we would need above what we had on hand. We also made a list of the furniture, including the car and the amount we could conceivably add to our savings if we were able to sell our stuff.

During this decision time, we took a trip with our friends, Ken and Glenda, to Stuttgart to meet friends of theirs who were serving with Navigators. It was an exciting time for all of us. Robert and Shiona quickly made new friends on the playground at the US air base where the Meeker family was living. They had a full, happy day playing outdoors, since there were no afternoon play time restrictions like they had to observe while living German style!

A day and a half seemed much too short for a visit with Dean and Irene. We soaked up the friendship and fellowship, but had to say goodbye. Robert and Shiona said sad goodbyes to new friends as we piled in the car and headed for home.

Jay and I started talking about our visit. He talked quite a bit with Dean, as I did with Irene. As we shared, we discovered we were both filled with compelling thoughts. Bursting to blurt out what was in our hearts, Jay says I spilled first.

I said, "While talking with Irene, it registered with me that a great deal of the furniture we would be selling or leaving behind, they could use."

Jay eagerly echoed my words as he had the same indication. We looked at each other in amazement and decided right then we wanted to give them whatever they could use, mentally ignoring our concern to sell our things in order to help pay our transportation to the states. When we shared this with Ken and Glenda they immediately volunteered to be responsible for the transporting of everything to Stuttgart. It was exciting for us to experience such rapid progress and direction about our plan to return home, even though these new developments seemed to by-pass our need for funds. Nevertheless, we didn't lose our zest with this unforeseen re-arrangement.

A few weeks later Ken and Glenda called, "Is it okay if we come over? We have something we want to share with you."

Our immediate response was, "Of course, come on over. We'll have coffee ready."

Sitting around the table, Ken reached in his pocket and pulled out an envelope.

"We just got this letter today and I want you to read it."

Ken has a quiet way about him, so we couldn't anticipate anything unusual. As Jay read the letter from Arizona, folks they described as casual friends, it went like this.

"You told us about your friends returning to the states. We've been praying for them. This check is for them. We just received our income tax refund and the Lord indicated to us that it is for your friends."

The check fell on the table. It was made out to Jay. We looked at it, we reached for our needs list and compared. Our financial needs were a secret between us and the Lord. There was no way these unknown-to-us folks could have known.

Looking at the check we saw the Lord's marvelous answer. The check matched our list almost to the pennies!

God was with us, with Dean and Irene in Stuttgart, and moving in the hearts of unknown friends. Our kids watched and listened in amazement and none of us have ever forgotten what the Lord Jesus did for us, for the Meekers, and for Ken and Glenda. There were so many blessings wrapped up in one big bundle, how could we sort it all out? All of us were partakers in what God was doing. We held hands, we prayed, and praised God for His faithfulness and His wonderful plans for all. Truly, it was a never to be forgotten experience.

The furniture arrived in Stuttgart and the Meeker family was thrilled. What we sent was just what they sorely needed. We were blessed again in being able to help, besides being blessed by the unexpected gift from Arizona, and we prayed blessings on the unknown friends in Arizona. God's ways include blessings all around! Many thanksgivings were given to our Father.

Living "Beyond the Fringes" doesn't mean we are special people. It's not about us, it is all about Him. It doesn't suggest that we are passed all trials and tests!

The day of our departure came. We traveled back to the states by way of Vancouver, B. C., where Shiona had a second grand mal seizure. Alarmed because the epilepsy was not yet confirmed or medicated, we were far from home and not knowing any doctor, sent us to our knees. (I don't think I will ever get passed the jitters). We prayed and yet again God was with us. He hadn't left; He is always with us, and brought us through another agonizing moment. Surely He would continue His care.

We began the journey south, leaving Jay in Portland, Oregon. We were praying he would find a new job with another company. The children and I went on to California to their grandparents. Before I could get Shiona to the pediatrician who cared for her from birth, she had her third grand mal seizure. Surely, the Lord has been with us always, again and again and again. He is always loving, giving courage, providing wisdom and guidance. We learned at this time to be more thankful for the wisdom and abilities given to doctors in their care of the human body. Certainly, medication is not the perfect answer, and it is always a balancing act between being helpful and causing unwanted side effects. So we trust in the Lord with all our heart, and lean not on our own understanding. In all our ways acknowledge Him; He will direct our paths (Proverbs 3:5-6).

The next step in our resettlement in the United States was our move to Portland where Jay located a new position. We left California to make the beautiful northwest our home. After smoggy California it wasn't hard to embrace the rain, fresh air, green growth all year, aromatic pine trees, fern, squirrels, deer, and meadows. Robert and Shiona started school, switching to English and making new friends. Neither of them ever complained about moves or changing schools. They both made friends easily, and enjoyed being able to tell about the different places where they had lived.

One day Robert popped in from school bursting with news.

"Hey, Mom, you gotta listen to this. I was at my locker getting my stuff ready for my next class, when the kid who has the locker next to me, looked at me in a curious way. Finally, he just blurted out, 'You know what? I know you. Yeah, I remember you!' I just kept looking at him, trying to figure it out. After a few minutes he explained, 'We met in Germany, at the US air base in Stuttgart. Don't you remember playing on the playground?' Then I started to remember. It was when we visited the Meekers. Isn't that wild? All the way from Germany and now we are both in Gladstone, Oregon! His name is Mike. He couldn't remember my name until I told him."

Truly astonished, they renewed their friendship, full-force, right then and there. Both were so excited. A gigantic move, a new school, and a friendship that went across the Atlantic and all the way to the other side of the United States can only be expressed as, Wow!

It wasn't long until we found a house to call our own, but what a surprise when Robert again brought the news.

"Hey, you guys, Mike and his family live right next door to us!"

The boys' friendship grew and they spent a lot of time together at Mike's house and at our house. We met his parents and confirmed this huge coincidence. It was several months later, when again, Robert came home after being with Mike. He had even greater news.

"You want to know what happened tonight?"

"Sure, Robert, what have you and Mike been up to that needs telling?"

"Well, this is really great! Mike and I have been talking about the Bible, and I've been telling him some things. He's been real interested, and tonight I introduced Mike to Jesus. I prayed something like this, 'Jesus, I want to introduce my friend, Mike. I've been telling him about You. He wants to know You and be part of Your family.' Then Mike prayed, too, and opened his heart to Jesus!"

Praising Jesus! That's what Robert was doing all evening—forget the homework! A casual friendship on the playground in Germany lasting not even two full days, yet the friendship skipped across the Atlantic, on to the west coast, to the middle school in the small town of Gladstone, Oregon, population less the 9,000 in 1977. Coincidence? No, never! God, our Majestic God, plans the way for us. He brings us in "Beyond the Fringes" to His just and holy ways!

For I know the plans I have for you. . . .plans for welfare and not for calamity to give you a future and a hope.

Then you will call upon Me and come and pray to Me, and I will listen to you. And you will seek Me and find Me, when you search for Me with all your heart. (Jeremiah 29:11-13)

*　*　*　*　*

Living Beyond the Fringes is living with your life in the Hands of the only True God, looking to Him, and finding your place in His peace. It is something we do daily, hourly, and it is necessary to keep that place clean with prayer and confession (especially when there are jitters).

Then my people will live in a peaceful habitation, and in secure dwellings and in undisturbed resting places. . . .O Lord, be gracious to us; we have waited for Thee. Be Thou our strength every morning, our salvation also in the time of distress. (Isaiah 32:18; 33:2)

One generation shall praise Thy works to another, and shall declare Thy mighty acts. They shall eagerly utter the memory of Thine abundant goodness, and shall shout joyfully of Thy righteousness. (Psalm 145:4, 7)

How can we not eagerly desire to declare His wondrous works, and praise His name to whomever will listen. We all have glorious memories we can mention about our gracious, merciful, and Majestic King when we live "Beyond the Fringes."

"In that circle of God's favor,
Circle of the Father's love;
(where) All is rest and rest forever,
All is perfectness above."

317

Perhaps you remember this old hymn of N. Denham Smith that reminds us of our eyes being full of wonder at His sacrifice that brings us beyond the fringe into His dwelling, the circle of the Father's love. Psalm 145 is an excellent place for remembering Who this God of our is. Place a marker there and read it frequently. It is all about His goodness!

My mouth will speak the praise of the Lord; and all flesh will bless His holy name forever and ever. (Psalm 145:7).

Jesus in Love and Mercy shine:
Take now this daily burden of mine.
I lay it down, You wore the crown.
Everlasting glory and honor be Thine

DEO GRATIAS
SOLI DEO GLORIA

We would love to hear from you:

Janet Muthmann
PO Box 28711
Kansas City, MO 64118-8711
janet459@att.net

Proceeds from book sales will be used to enable
Christian organizations working with and for
the disabled.

CPSIA information can be obtained at www.ICGtesting.com
Printed in the USA
LVOW01s0735260813

349602LV00003B/4/P